Tom Cruise

Anatomy of an Actor

CAHIERS DU
CINEMA

Tom Cruise

Amy Nicholson

Introduction

"I was always a very serious person. I was never very frivolous. I did things I wanted to do well and took pride in them."[1]
—Tom Cruise, 1990

The role was a high-school kid desperate to lose his virginity. A friend suggests a hooker, and over the course of a crazy weekend the innocent boy falls—temporarily, at least—for the older woman who takes him to bed. His agent said he'd be a fool to turn down the part. It would be his first starring gig, teen sex comedies were a huge market, and frankly the twenty-year-old bit player was in no position to say no. So Tom Cruise said yes. And the decision defined the rest of his career.

The film was *Losin' It* (1983), and Cruise was embarrassed by it before it even hit theaters, where it made a miniscule $1.26 million. He didn't do press—he didn't even go to the premiere. Less than a year later, he openly groaned it was "a gross mistake I won't make again."[2] He hasn't. Just two years into his career, Tom Cruise made a vow that he has never broken. "I learned a great lesson in doing that movie. I realized that not everybody is capable of making good films,"[3] said Cruise. "I decided after *Losin' It*, I only wanted to work with the best people."[4] He has.

Steven Spielberg, Stanley Kubrick, Ridley Scott, Tony Scott, Paul Thomas Anderson, Cameron Crowe, Francis Ford Coppola, Martin Scorsese, Oliver Stone, Brian De Palma, Ron Howard, Michael Mann, Edward Zwick, Franco Zeffirelli, Barry Levinson, Christopher McQuarrie, Brad Bird, Rob Reiner, Sydney Pollack, J. J. Abrams, John Woo, Ben Stiller, Robert Redford. Between them, Tom Cruise's directors have racked up seventy-nine Academy Award nominations.

Cruise himself has earned three Oscar nods—and lost. Therein lies the great paradox of his career. In the three decades since *Losin' It*, he's become—and remained—the box office's biggest international star. Globally, his films have scored over $8 billion dollars. Though he's adored by audiences and the most talented directors of his generation, one thing continues to elude Tom Cruise: respect.

He's been a Nazi, a paraplegic, an assassin, a redneck, a car salesman, a samurai warrior, and a drunk. He's played vampires and hustlers and Irishmen and elves. Despite his efforts, Tom Cruise's image hasn't changed. He's still misread as a one-note hero who relies on his charm—even though his characters haven't grinned in a decade. Never has an actor been so closely watched, yet so rarely seen—so successful while still struggling for recognition.

"I have never thought it was as simple as just smiling through a movie," said Cruise.[5] "I've had to work extra hard at everything I've done."[6]

Cruise dedicates himself completely to his roles. He has taught himself to play pool, fly planes, drive race cars, flip bottles, and sing. He's dangled from the tallest building in the world, suffered months in a wheelchair, and locked himself away for two claustrophobic years working with the secretive Stanley Kubrick. He even trained underwater to blow a single air bubble out of his nose so Steven Spielberg wouldn't have to add it digitally in post. Explained Cruise, "My drive and determination go back to different times as a kid. I had to set goals and force myself to be disciplined because I always felt I had barriers to overcome."[7]

Humble Beginnings

Thomas Cruise Mapother IV was born on July 3, 1962 in Syracuse, New York, the only son among four children. His father, Thomas Cruise Mapother III, was an engineer and inventor. His mother, Mary Lee, was a stay-at-home mom who loved the theater. The family was nomadic. Cruise changed schools fifteen times in twelve years to keep pace with his father's restless career. At six-two, his dad towered over the small-for-his-age boy—and he made sure his son felt it. "He was a bully and a coward," said Cruise, "the kind of person where, if something goes wrong, they kick you."[8]

When Cruise was twelve, his father abandoned the family in Ottawa, Canada, and refused to pay child support. The boy and his sisters moved again to Louisville, Kentucky, where he took part-time jobs to keep the family afloat. Cruise would deliver papers before school, daydream during his classes, and take out his aggressions in after-school sports.

"I was always looking for attention. I'd get into fights, get suspended from school," recalled Cruise. "I think it was out of a need to be creative."[9] A bright but mediocre student due to his undiagnosed dyslexia, he felt most comfortable on the field. Even for an athlete, Cruise had incredible physical control. It helped that, thanks to his roving childhood, he'd practiced every sport

Tom Cruise in Edward Zwick's
The Last Samurai (2003).

because he knew it was the quickest way to fit
in. If baseball was popular, he'd pick up a bat. If
it was ice hockey or football, he'd master them,
too. Cruise was motivated and adaptable—two
qualities that would drive his later career, and ones
he'd honed ever since he was four years old, when
he'd refuse to come in for dinner until he could
manage to hit a line drive.

"If I could just focus in and do something,
I know I've got the energy and creativity to be
great," said Cruise.[10] When he was seventeen,
he thought he'd settled on it: wrestling. He was
now a senior in Glen Ridge, New Jersey, where
his family had resettled after his mother married
a plastics salesman named Jack South. The key
competitions at his newest school took place on the
mat, where the lean, tough Cruise was a natural.
With graduation just months away, he dreamed of
getting a college wrestling scholarship, maybe even
making it to the Olympics. And then he pulled a
tendon in his knee, an injury that sidelined him for
the rest of the season.

Devastated, Cruise decided to distract himself by
auditioning for the school musical, *Guys and Dolls*.
He won the lead, slick gangster Nathan Detroit, a
part played by everyone from Frank Sinatra to Bob
Hoskins. Theater was a lark. But that first opening
night changed everything.

"It was just an incredible experience to see what
we felt was a lot of talent coming forth all of a
sudden," said Mary Lee. "It had been dormant for

so many years—not thought of or talked about or
discussed in any way."[11] Cruise was transformed by
the applause. That night, he asked his mother and
Jack for their blessing to pursue an acting career.
He made them a deal: give him ten years to try, and
if he hadn't made it in a decade, he'd abandon the
idea and get practical. They agreed.

Cruise skipped graduation, lopped off his
father's last name, and moved to New York with
nothing but a busted lime green Ford Pinto he'd
purchased for fifty bucks, an $850 loan from
his stepfather, and his personal promise that he
would be a millionaire before he was thirty. He
found jobs busing tables and serving ice cream,
and he discovered a manager through a classmate
who'd done some TV. He quickly realized the
manager was worthless. "She had me read this
Hershey's commercial, and, you know, it was one
of these, 'Yeah, yeah, yeah, babe, you're beautiful,
I'm going to make you a star' sort of situations,"
said Cruise. "She'd ask me to run errands or go
grocery shopping for her."[12] Downbeat but not
disillusioned, he then found a lawyer to help him
break their five-year contract.

He met an agent, and the agent got him a few
auditions. He did *Godspell* in a New Jersey church
and was rejected from the TV pilot of *Fame*. (The
casting director thought he was too "intense"
and not "pretty enough."[13]) Then he stumbled in,
hungover, to test for Franco Zeffirelli's *Endless
Love* (1981), a schmaltzy Brooks Shields vehicle

Opposite: As Cadet Captain
David Shawn in Harold
Becker's *Taps* (1981).

Tom Cruise, Timothy Hutton,
and Sean Penn on the set
of *Taps*.

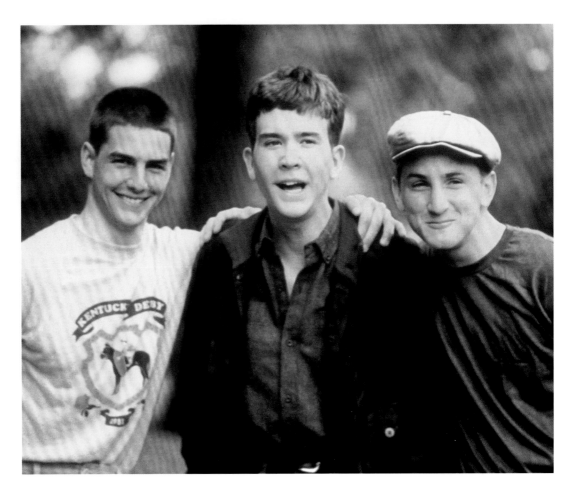

most famous for its Diana Ross and Lionel Richie titular duet… and for giving Cruise his first break. Zeffirelli cast him as a half-nude teen arsonist. Cruise was onscreen for less than one minute, but he'd been given a Hollywood stamp of approval. The film came out exactly two weeks after his nineteenth birthday. Tom Cruise was on his way.

From Bit Parts to Superstardom

Next, he won a small part in Harold Becker's *Taps* (1981)—a smaller part than people realize. In the final film, he plays a minor creep named David Shawn who shoots up his school with a machine gun. But Cruise wasn't cast as David Shawn—he was cast in the even more minor part of David Shawn's sidekick. Still, Cruise took his role seriously, shaving his head and packing on pounds of muscle. Cruise was "200 percent there," said *Taps* star Sean Penn. "Good acting, but so far in the intense direction that it was funny." Director Becker noticed. Before shooting got under way, he asked Cruise if he'd be willing to replace the original David Shawn. Cruise was shocked—and not in a good way. "If this isn't all right with the other actor, I don't want to do it," he told the producer. He was driven, but he wasn't conniving, and was convinced to take the promotion only when told that if he didn't step into the part, someone else would. Joked Penn, "Cruise was so strong that the other guy didn't have a chance."[14]

"I remember sitting in that hotel room looking up at the ceiling and thinking, 'This is it. This is the turning point of my life,'" said Cruise of filming *Taps*. "I felt that this was going to show, to me, 'Can I do anything? Do I have talent or not?' That's a scary proposition, because I felt I don't know what I'm going to do. I'm just going to give it everything I have because I love this and I want to be able to get good at this."[15] In the press material for *Taps*, his first-ever published biography, the then-nineteen-year-old Cruise listed his hobbies as jogging, reading, and making miniature remote control models of boats. "Acting has helped me mature," he said. "I don't know my limits as an actor yet."[16]

When *Taps* was over, Cruise told his agent that he was finished auditioning for commercials and TV. "I wanted to make movies," he insisted, and so his agent pushed him into one: *Losin' It*. After that disaster, he learned to say no. At a career point when most young actors with his scant credits—one line in Zeffirelli's *Endless Love*, a supporting part in *Taps*, and a flop—would have said yes to a toothpaste commercial, he said no to horror movies, lame comedies, and $70,000 offers even when he wasn't sure he'd ever get another job. "He thought I was out of my mind to say no," said Cruise of his agent.[17] So he fired his agent and replaced him with CAA newbie Paula Wagner, insisting, "I'd rather not work than do bad films."[18]

Over the next three decades, Cruise and Wagner's partnership turned him into the biggest actor in the world. Teenaged Tom Cruise had promised to give his dreams ten years. He had a star on the Walk of Fame in five.

Tom Cruise's career is at once calculatedly modern and curiously old-fashioned. He launched his own production company and was the first actor to insist on promoting his films abroad. Yet he's rejected trends, shunned sequels, and still reads his own scripts. Starting with the fifth film on his résumé—the star-making *Risky Business* (1983)—he's taken a strong hand in developing his own characters even when outranked by his legendary directors. And when his fame superseded every director in the business, he cold-called young talents and asked them to write him a good part so his clout could help get their films made. "No kid thinks he's going to be President of the United States, and no kid thinks he's going to get Tom Cruise in his movie," [19] laughed Sundance wunderkind Paul Thomas Anderson, who would direct Cruise in *Magnolia* (1999). "A movie star like Tom Cruise was, I thought, out of my reach." [20]

"I make the decisions, I pick the scripts, I have only myself to blame if things don't work out," insisted Cruise. "That is the way I want to live my life. That is the way I set out to live it from the beginning." [21]

Throughout his career, he's leaned on the tough lessons learned as a child. After *Top Gun* (1986) turned him into Hollywood's cash cow, instead of chasing a big, lucrative career, Cruise knew to stay calm and think smart. "I went, 'Uh, oh, be careful,'" he recalled. "You realize that there are people around you can't trust. I knew from being around my father, who hurt people, that not everyone means you well." [22]

Real-Life Parallels

Father issues haunt his films—additions he's had written into the scripts. In Cruise's films, fathers disappear but leave a legacy that strangles their sons: *Top Gun*, *Magnolia*, *Rain Man* (1988), *Days of Thunder* (1990), *A Few Good Men* (1992), *Vanilla Sky* (2001). Even father figures—*The Firm* (1993), *Mission: Impossible* (1996), *Eyes Wide Shut* (1999), *Minority Report* (2002)—can't be trusted. By the age of forty-three, when Tom Cruise was one year older than his dad had been when he left the family, he was playing his own bad father in Spielberg's *War of the Worlds* (2005) and processing the pain in a different way. When Cruise's character, Ray Ferrier, plays an awkward game of catch with his estranged son, the moment echoes Cruise's memory of tossing a baseball with his own dad moments after he had announced he was leaving him and the family.

The parallels are striking only because Cruise has otherwise worked so hard to separate his personal life from his onscreen image—a challenge he's found increasingly difficult in the tabloid era. Pick up an article about the actor and you're more likely to read about his three marriages, three children, and religious beliefs than his craft. Yet Cruise continues to strive for excellence, seeking out and hurdling emotional and physical dares, even when critics won't notice.

"His road was never paved. It was always full of potholes and he jumped over them all," said *Top Gun*'s Don Simpson, the first big producer to write a role with Tom Cruise in mind. [23] "He believes anything is possible. That's the key to Tom Cruise." [24]

Craft and Calculation

During the promotional barnstorming for each new film, Cruise insists that it's the most challenging role of his career. The boast is half hype, but he also needs it to be true. In retrospect, it's hard to remember that many of his early hits were a risk: *Top Gun* was expected to be blasted off screens by Sylvester Stallone's *Cobra* (1986); his bold Oscar leap *Born on the Fourth of July* (1989) was predicted to be jeered by critics. And Cruise's controversial casting as the bloodsucker Lestat in *Interview with the Vampire* (1994) had author Anne Rice so angry that she publicly denounced him and the actor received death threats.

"I like feeling nervous and excited about my roles," said Cruise. "Once I've done something, I don't want to do it again. That just bores me." [25]

Anatomy of an Actor: Tom Cruise tracks the superstar's smartest and most perilous choices, the roles that could have derailed his career but instead defined it. It's a study of craft and calculation, of Hollywood's most powerful underdog still chasing the respect he's more than earned.

"I want to be able to look back and say I've pushed it as far as I could," said Cruise. "I've made some damn big mistakes, and I look like an asshole a lot of the time. But I did some good stuff, too." [26]

1

Joel Goodsen

Risky Business (1983)
Paul Brickman

"Sometimes you've gotta say, 'What the fuck,'
and make your move."
—Joel Goodsen

"We have a major new talent on our hands,"
wrote the *Reader*'s Dan Sallitt in his gushing
review of *Risky Business*.[27] He didn't mean Tom
Cruise. He meant *Risky Business*'s writer and
director, Paul Brickman, a thirty-four-year-old
first-time filmmaker whose only credits to date
were the scripts for the CB radio comedy *Handle
with Care* (1977) and the Bad News Bears sequel
The Bad News Bears in Breaking Training
(1977). As for the star of *Risky Business*, Sallitt
didn't find him worth mentioning.

Brickman deserved applause. He'd tirelessly
shopped his sex comedy about a teenager who
opens a brothel in his parents' suburban home
to every studio in town—Warner Bros., Fox,
CBS Theatrical Films—all of whom dismissed
it as a knock-off of *Porky's* (1982), the R-rated
high school flick that raised eyebrows when
it raked in $111.3 million. But *Risky Business*
wasn't just another virginity romp—it was
a stylish riff on eighties materialism and
an extension of Brickman's own childhood
watching his father, Morrie, skewer greed in
his syndicated comic strip *The Small Society*.
Risky Business wanted to question capitalism
in a sexy, young dramedy that wouldn't lecture
Reaganomics-bred teenagers. But first, Brickman
had to cast the perfect all-American boy to play
Joel Goodsen, a kid who travels an arc from
innocence to corruption. Brickman needed a
young actor who could be both shy and soft and
charismatic and calculating. And he knew who
he didn't want: Tom Cruise.

The Reluctant Sociopath

Today, that seems surprising, but when
Brickman cast *Risky Business* in 1982, it's
remarkable that he knew who Tom Cruise was
at all. An unknown nineteen-year-old with
three films on his résumé, Cruise was practically
invisible—and audiences who remembered his
face assumed he was a psycho. Cruise spoke
his first onscreen words in a forty-seven-second
cameo in *Endless Love*, a gloppy romance
directed by Franco Zeffirelli. They were

memorable—he advises a heartbroken boyfriend
to burn down his ex-girlfriend's house.

"Eight years old and I was into arson. No,
I'm serious. I lit a whole pile of newspapers—
you ever try to light a whole pile of wet
newspapers?" squeaks Cruise, sprawling
boldly in front of the camera wearing nothing
but running shoes and tiny shorts. "You want
to hear the wild part? It's like I'm a hero or
something. They think I saved the whole block!"
As Cruise collapses into maniacal giggles, his
friend bikes away and sets a fire on his ex's
porch. Then *Endless Love* gets even more glum.
The lesson: Never trust Tom Cruise.

Cruise played another sociopath in his second
film, *Taps*. Cruise's military school cadet David
Shawn is a war-mongering zealot who loves
to stalk the halls of his prestigious academy
swinging a saber. When his fellow students
seize control of their campus and blunder into
a deadly standoff with the police, stars Timothy
Hutton and Sean Penn try to restore order. But
it's Cruise, almost unrecognizable with his thick
neck and shaved head, whose lust for blood
and power turns him into the film's secondary
villain. In his first scene, Cruise charms Hutton
while giving Penn the middle finger. In his final
scene, Cruise crouches fiendishly over a machine
gun while screaming, "It's beautiful, man—it's
beautiful!" at the carnage he's creating. ("We'd
all kind of laugh, because it was so sincere,"
joked Penn.[28]) The unhinged cadet put Cruise
on the casting agents' radar—but only for other
nutcase roles. "After *Taps* came out I was offered
every horror film, every killer-murderer part,"
groaned Cruise.[29] The jobs would have paid the
teenager more money than he'd ever seen. But
Cruise didn't want to be another crazy character
actor. He wanted to be a star. So he held out for a
lead role, and took the first one he was offered: as
the virgin who romances Shelley Long in the ill-
fated *Losin' It*. The terrible teen comedy remains
the lowest-grossing, worst-reviewed film of his
career. But it had two positive outcomes: first,
no one saw it, and second, Cruise fired his agent.
"I have to work with good people and good
directors and grow," the young actor resolved.
Combining the clout of his new rep, CAA's
Paula Wagner, and his friendship with Sean
Penn, Cruise wheedled a minor role as rebellious

The incomparable Joel
Goodsen in Paul Brickman's
Risky Business (1983).

EUROGROUP Films présente

AMERICAN TEENAGERS

redneck Steve Randle in Francis Ford Coppola's all-star, heartthrob production of *The Outsiders* (1983) "I just went to Francis and said, 'Look, I don't care what role you give me, I really want to work with you,'" pleaded Cruise. "'I want to be there with all these young actors.'"[30]

The Outsiders, a rough-and-tumble teen drama about a war between the dirty Greasers and the posh Socs, was set and shot in Tulsa, Oklahoma. Having one of the film's smallest roles, Cruise was determined to stand out. He removed the cap from his chipped front tooth (the result of a childhood hockey accident), refused to shower for most of the nine-week shoot, and opened the flick chasing a car like a frenzied, rabid dog. Wrote costar Rob Lowe of his first impression of the not-yet-superstar, "He's open, friendly, funny, and has an almost robotic, bloodless focus and an intensity that I've never encountered before."[31]

Landing the Part

Still, compared to *Taps*' David Shawn, *The Outsiders*' Steve Randle was too small a character to keep him on the map. Everything depended on Cruise's next move—and when he heard about Brickman's sophisticated but sellable *Risky Business*, he vowed to win the lead. Though dyslexic, he was smart enough to see the script's complexity—and

commercialism. "It was such a well-written screenplay," realized Cruise, and he begged Wagner to get him an audition.[32]

No luck. Brickman refused to give Cruise a shot. He'd seen *Taps* and huffed, "This guy's a killer! Let him do *Amityville 3*!"[33] Besides, Cruise had already played a virgin with a fondness for hookers—and that movie had flopped. Why saddle his own passion project with Cruise's bad karma? But Wagner was determined and crafty. She made a secret deal with one of the Brickman's office mates to casually invite her and Cruise to drop by. Cruise knocked on Brickman's door, flashed him his trademark grin, and scored a screen test.

Smelly and shaggy from still shooting *The Outsiders*, Cruise made an impression. "I'll never forget that audition," said producer Jon Avnet. "I had never seen an actor do what Tom did in that first audition where he would make a choice, make another choice, make another choice, and then be open to anything you had to say. Everybody was so stunned in the room because he had the chipped tooth."[34] Despite looking nothing like a normal suburban teenager, he managed to convince Brickman and Avnet that he understood Joel's vulnerability, and assured them that even if they couldn't see past his current greaser gear, he'd totally transform himself by the time he appeared on set. If, that is, they gave him a chance.

Michael J. Fox, Tom Hanks, and Nicolas Cage all auditioned for Joel Goodsen, but it was Cruise who got called back for a chemistry test with costar Rebecca De Mornay. *The Outsiders* was on a night shooting schedule, so Cruise took the redeye to LA, slipped on a preppy Adidas pullover, and tried to convince De Mornay, a posh European-bred beauty, that he wasn't a scumbag. De Mornay wasn't impressed. "We didn't test that well," admitted Cruise. But he still got the part. "Paul just believed in me."[35] In this raw teenager, Brickman saw determination, innocence, and heat. Plus, he was stricken by the former athlete's physical command, spotting that Cruise had "an innate talent in the way he moves and expresses himself."[36]

As a well-earned reward for Cruise's dirty devotion to *The Outsiders*, Francis Ford Coppola had already offered him a slightly larger part in his next film, *Rumble Fish* (1983). Now Cruise had to say no. "Here's the director of *Apocalypse Now, The Conversation,* and *The Godfather*," am turning him down to do this movie about hookers.'" During his stumbling explanation to the five-time Oscar-winning filmmaker, Cruise realized *Risky Business* risked being underestimated. "I remember looking at Francis Ford Coppola's face as I was saying, 'Well, it's about this guy, who… Well, this call girl… Well, this is what the story is, but it's not really what it's about… and he runs a brothel out of his home… but it's really good.'"[37]

Creating the Character

Though Oklahoma and Illinois are only one state away, culturally Steve Randle and Joel Goodsen were one million miles apart. With the part his, Cruise said good-bye to *The Outsiders* gang and flew to Florida to transform himself into a coddled Chicago teenager. First, he sweated off fourteen pounds by jogging and dieting. Then he gorged on junk food to bury his muscles under a layer of soft fat so that Joel's pecs would jiggle babyishly when he padded around the house in white briefs. "'He's a very vulnerable person,' explained Tom. 'I didn't want any physical defenses up for him. No muscle armor at all.'"[38]

The next step was deciding on Goodsen's wardrobe with costumer Ilene Giardini. "I gave him a pinched-cheek, suburban look. Dressed him like his mother dressed him," said Cruise, who starts the story in a button-up and smothering sweater that choke his throat.[39] Joel's clothes subtly but deliberately set him apart from his friends. When the boys smoke cigars around a poker table, Curtis Armstrong's rumpled camouflage jacket and Bronson Pinchot's breezy polo shirt contrast with Cruise's suffocating layers. Though Cruise is the handsomest of the gang, he looks uncomfortably, untouchably young, like a choirboy who snuck away from Sunday school to hang out with the big kids—it isn't until long after he gets laid that he slips into his iconic black tee and sports coat.

With Joel Goodsen's perfectly trimmed hair, white teeth, and prim clothing, twenty-one-year-old Tom Cruise was the face of upper-middle-class privilege. It wasn't a natural fit. Though Cruise was born into relative comfort with the dynastic name Thomas Cruise Mapother IV, at twelve, he was forced to grow up fast when his father, Thomas Cruise Mapother III, abandoned the family. To help support his mother and three sisters, Cruise worked part-time jobs throughout middle and high school, delivering newspapers and handing over his earnings. To save money on Christmas, the Mapother clan gave each other poems instead of presents. "For me at that age, it *was* 'What the fuck,'" said Cruise, "although I had a very different kind of childhood."[40] Joel would disappoint his parents if he didn't get into Princeton, but for Cruise college was barely on the table. While he graduated from the posh Glen Ridge High School in 1980, Cruise claims he never fit in with the wealthy kids. "They didn't have the childhood I had, and I didn't feel like they'd understand me," he said.[41] But he did study them—and his research proved invaluable for shaping Joel Goodsen.

Cruise knew he had to do more than just memorize his lines and show up. His future hinged on *Risky Business*. If the movie was great, he could follow in the footsteps of Dustin Hoffman after *The Graduate*. If it was awful, having two leading flops in a row meant his career might be over before it began. "I was absolutely worried about if I'd be able to deliver for everyone," said Cruise. "There were sleepless nights." So while Cruise was unfailingly polite on set, he was also outspoken about his concerns, even calling Brickman at three o'clock in the morning from a diner when worried about nailing his big "What the fuck" speech the next day. (Grumbled Brickman, "I'm sleeping. We'll go over it in the morning."[42]) Later, Cruise's intense behind-the-scenes involvement would trigger gossip that he'd tried to get De Mornay fired, rumors that dogged him even after the two became a couple.

Restraint

Consider what happens to Joel Goodsen in *Risky Business*—he's surprised at home by a transvestite escort, he loses his virginity to a prostitute, his father's Porsche plunges into a lake, he's suspended from school, his entire house is held for ransom by a pimp named Guido—and it's remarkable how Cruise consistently steers clear of predicable reactions. He doesn't throw

tantrums. Instead, he channels his panic inward. In the moments where his panic slips out, say in the scene where Joel desperately grabs the school nurse by the lapels to give him an excuse for missing two midterms, it's a controlled miscalculation, not a reckless lashing out. You'd expect the main character of a sex comedy to lead with his crotch—like, say, *Losin' It*'s Jackie Earle Haley, who spends the film howling like a horny wolf. But Tom Cruise makes a drastically different physical choice. Joel is paralytically stiff and silent. He's obsessed with sex, but he can't rouse himself to actually have it. "He was a very sexual character, but he also had that ingenuousness," pinpointed Cruise.[43] Joel is so divorced from his own body that when a naked girl invites him into the shower in *Risky Business*'s opening dream sequence, not only does Cruise's nervous face silently contradict his claim to be thrilled, he doesn't even do his own talking. Instead, he lip-synchs to his own voice-over, mouthing along as his subconscious asks the babe what she'd like him to do.

Joel is scared of everything: of his "girlfriend" Lana, of her pimp, of failing his SATs, and of failing his parents. He can't even masturbate without picturing his parents calling the cops. In turn, Brickman shoots Joel like a captive, continually framing him behind bars, from the shadows of his window blinds to a gated peephole that covers his face. Cruise quickly picked up on Brickman's subtle camerawork and started adding his own character details. Cruise keeps him physically constrained, a prisoner of his own anxieties. As Lana first walks into his house, he can't even rouse himself to stand—when the camera cuts to the girl posing by his window, we're almost surprised when Joel summons the nerve to walk into the frame. "I did feel room to create and play," said Cruise.[44] In the scene where Joel first calls Lana for a date, the script called for him to sprawl on the floor and feign confidence. But when Lana presses him for his name and location, Joel freezes. While the cameras rolled, Cruise surprised Brickman by slipping a baseball catcher's mask over his face, as though Joel could only summon the courage by pretending to be someone else entirely, and then ad-libbed that his name was "Ralph." Brickman struggled not to laugh and managed to keep the take.

The audience is invited to empathize with Joel when things are awkward, but almost never when things are fun—in *Risky Business*, even the fun rarely feels like fun. Whenever Cruise cuts loose, Brickman forces us to watch him from an almost anthropological remove. Gunning his father's Porsche for a drag race, Joel doesn't take us along on his joyride. Instead, the camera pulls back as he leaves us behind. Even when Joel restlessly spins the sports car in doughnuts, the camera stares down at him from a belittling aerial shot with as much interest as someone watching an ant drag a leaf.

We can't even enjoy watching Joel have sex. Cruise's love scenes with De Mornay have an art-house aloofness. The camera peers from around a wall as they hump on the stairs, then pans to child photographs of Cruise himself to kill the erotic buzz. When Brickman finally cuts back to their tryst, Cruise is now completely hidden between a high-backed chair, and our attention is drawn to the American flag waving on the television. We're finally allowed close to the action during the infamous L-train encounter, but only temporarily. After an extended beat, the camera escapes the intimacy of the train and heads outside to watch Joel and Lana pass us by again and again in a blur.

Movement

But Cruise's and Brickman's restraint highlights the rare moments when Joel Goodsen finally *moves*. There's his loose-limbed panic trying to push the Porsche back to dry land, his frantic sprint to school after Lana makes him late for a quiz, and a moment in the gym when he body-slams Curtis Armstrong, the friend who upended his life. ("This is where you really knew what you were doing," joked Brickman to the former high-school wrestler. "That was an easy day."[45]) As his personal favorite physical beat, Brickman points to Joel swaggering into the kitchen the morning after his second night with Lana. While the beautiful blonde makes his breakfast wearing nothing but his Princeton sweatshirt, it suddenly dawns on him that her services might cost him another dollar. Watch Cruise's left earlobe: it sags an eighth of an inch—a move that subconsciously recalls a sad puppy. "I was thinking about the scene the night before, and I thought, 'If I could get my left ear to go down…'" admitted Cruise,[46] and even though the detail is easy to miss even if looking for it, he practiced the ear drop in the mirror until he had it right.

Risky Business's most famous physical moment is its most legendary scene: Joel's giddy, pants-less dance to Bob Seger's "Old Time Rock and Roll." Brickman sets up the moment long before Cruise skids across the floor in white tube socks. Armstrong's loutish character has pressured Joel to take advantage of his freedom while his folks are on vacation. But Joel doesn't quite know how—his idea of savagery is eating a TV dinner. Then he pours himself five fingers of Chivas Regal. In the next scene, when he cranks up the stereo and cuts loose, Joel hasn't discovered rebellion—he's just drunk.

The choreography was entirely Cruise's invention. Brickman's script said merely: "Joel dances in underwear through the house," and in rehearsal the director simply told him to get loose while taking note of the moves he liked.

"I used to dance around my living room to this song before," joked Cruise of his preparation. "This and Michael Jackson."[47] Today, we see the scene as the highpoint of eighties cool. But look closer at Cruise's choices and it's clear Joel is just a wasted nerd. What Cruise passes off as coolness—his rock star strut, the popped collar, the thrusting fireplace poker at his crotch, the splits—he deliberately tosses aside when he belly flops on the couch and writhes like a dying cockroach. In the morning when he sobers up, nothing has changed—it will take more than a shimmy to shake him alive.

That dance defined *Risky Business*. But Brickman's heart was in the scene immediately after when Joel and his friends talk about their futures. Everyone agrees they want a high-paying job, but when the table turns to Joel, he insists he wants to "serve my fellow mankind." Cruise delivers the line ambiguously—we can't tell if he's sincere or sarcastic. Later, Cruise would insist that "Joel—and not Rebecca De Mornay's character—may be the real prostitute."[48] But audiences missed the message. They swooned over Cruise's cool Ray-Bans and deemed *Risky Business* a celebration of commercialism. After all, who *would* want to be that Future Entrepreneur classmate of Joel Goodsen's who made just $500 dollars selling decorative planters when Joel's brothel haul was $8,000 in one night? The movie's executive producer, music mogul David Geffen, didn't like Brickman's dour denouement where Joel loses the girl, gets rejected from Princeton, and breaks his mom's crystal egg. Geffen forced Brickman to give the film an upbeat ending, spilling so much bad blood in the process that *Risky Business* didn't even have a premiere—not even a cast and crew screening. Soured, Brickman would direct only one more film before retiring to write.

A Box Office Success

Three decades on, *Risky Business* seems a sure bet. But it didn't that summer. In advertisements, *Risky Business* looked like just another teensploitation comedy shoehorned into the dumping ground of August. But something about the film itself—the slick Tangerine Dream soundtrack, the cold eroticism, that new kid Tom Cruise—clicked. Even opening on just 670 screens—half the theaters of its competition—*Risky Business* launched onto the box office charts at number three. By the end of the month, distributor Warner Bros. smartened up and expanded the flick into wide release. It would become the tenth highest-grossing film of 1983.

Few film critics recognized that Cruise—not Brickman—would be the breakout talent of *Risky Business*. Reviews mentioned the actor as an afterthought, like he was merely another prop in Brickman's highly stylized teen movie.

"I read a review of my dance number in *Risky Business* that somehow failed to talk about my work," sighed Cruise. "After I'd worked so hard to create a character, that was frustrating."[49] Only a handful recognized that this young Cruise kid might have something. "He occupies this movie the way Dustin Hoffman occupied *The Graduate*," crowed Roger Ebert, adding that Cruise "knows how to imply a whole world by what he won't say, can't feel, and doesn't understand."[50] The *Village Voice* offered this unintentionally funny kudos: "Tom Cruise, one of the villainous WASPs in the greaser-oriented *The Outsiders*, breaks out of the pack in *Risky Business* with a gracefully self-mocking performance"[51]—apparently, Cruise had sold his suburban teen so well that the *Voice*, which must not have actually seen *The Outsiders*, assumed he'd played one of the slick rich kids instead of a country thug. Others were less enthused. The sharp-tongued Pauline Kael joked that Cruise was "like a shorter Christopher Reeve, and the film seems to be raising the question, 'Can nice boys be sexy?'"[52] while the *New Republic* shrugged: "The boy, Tom Cruise, isn't very appealing."[53] David Denby of *New York* magazine, who disliked the film, vented his aggression on its leading man, sighing, "A standard-issue baby-faced actor, Cruise has a slight, undeveloped voice and a nervous smile, which he relies on whenever the script reveals one of its innumerable holes."[54]

But when *Risky Business* became a sleeper hit, the publicity about-faced. Teenagers loved Tom Cruise—and therefore, so did Hollywood. By the end of the month, Tom Cruise was singled out in the *LA Times* as one of the "Summer's Hottest Faces" alongside Matthew Broderick, Nicolas Cage, Ally Sheedy, Jennifer Beals, and Rob Lowe. "He comes across as a very together, solid young man," observed a casting director. "You get a lot of compassion from him. You care about him."[55]

Celebrity puff pieces popped up in outlets as diverse as *People* magazine, *Rolling Stone*, *Tiger Beat*, and *Playboy*. Fans deemed Cruise their new favorite heartthrob, but the would-be serious actor wasn't interested in playing along. Though his face was everywhere, Cruise himself kept a low profile. In interviews, he distilled his biography to a few key details—his dyslexia, his athleticism, his rootless upbringing—that sketched a loose portrait of a humble, lonely, and approachable outsider while leaving enough blank space to allow audiences to fill in whatever they wanted to imagine. Only one year had passed since Cruise resolved to reject psycho roles and cheap teen comedies. Now he again showed the preternatural confidence of a young actor determined to become a major name. By the time the Golden Globes nominated him for Best Actor in a Musical or Comedy (he lost), Cruise was officially one of the most sought-after

Just a wasted nerd: Tom Cruise in the film's most famous scene.

Following pages: Joel Goodsen in panic mode with Lena (Rebecca de Mornay) and her colleague, Vicki (Shera Danese).

"This guy's already showing traits that will make him famous; he's zeroed in like a laser—all business and very intense," thought Rob Lowe of Tom Cruise during auditions for *The Outsiders*.[a] Though they'd become friends during the shoot, sometimes even sharing a bed under orders from Francis Ford Coppola, they were young, competitive, and determined to spin their small parts into serious careers. In his autobiography, *Stories I Only Tell My Friends*, Lowe describes nineteen-year-old Cruise's striking concentration and commitment to character.

It's 110 degrees in this sweatbox of a studio as Tom Cruise is called to the floor. Now I have real issues; he's giving my scene a try. He begins Sodapop's big breakdown scene at the end of the movie. I watch him and think, that's it, I'm done. He's clearly a force to be reckoned with, and is more focused and ambitious than I ever thought about being. (And that's saying something.)
But then… Tom has stopped. Stopped the scene! Right in the middle of the monologue! A hush falls over the room.
"Um, I'm sorry. Um, I'm really sorry," he says, looking directly at Francis. "This just isn't working for me."
Holy shit! Not working for him? I thought Francis Ford Coppola was the judge of what works and what doesn't. There is a low murmur among the actors. Francis lets him try again. When he's done, I know the Cruise missile threat has passed. […]
The consensus is that Cruise is taking a chance with Risky Business. The script is funny, but dark and weird; the director wrote it himself and has no experience. […] I do manage to spend time with Cruise, who is shooting Risky Business in town (the night I visit, they are filming the iconic Porsche-going-into-Lake-Michigan scene), but since both of us are so busy, it isn't the same. Also, Tom has a new perspective on his acting style, telling me, "I want to spend time hanging with you but Joel [his character] doesn't."

Opposite: Bad boys in Francis Ford Coppola's *Outsiders* (1982): Tom Cruise, Rob Lowe, C. Thomas Howell, Matt Dillon, Ralph Macchio, Emilio Estevez, and Patrick Swayze.

Right: The new-look Joel Goodsen.

faces in Hollywood. But instead of burnishing his fame by following the expected script of nightclub escapades and tabloids—like, say, best friend Sean Penn, who two years later married the pop star Madonna—Cruise realized there was a second way to stardom: stepping back and seizing control of his image. He stopped doing publicity altogether, telling the studio, "I'm just not personally ready to do this."[56]

At twenty-one, Tom Cruise was getting serious. "My craft is the most important thing in my life," he insisted.[57] The second most important was his agent Paula Wagner, whose persistence had transformed him from a crazy character actor to a newly formed star. "It's like I'm handling Paul Newman right now," Wagner told the *LA Times*. "Right now, we're building a firm foundation for a career."[58]

2

Maverick

Top Gun (1986)
Tony Scott

"I feel the need, the need for speed."
—Maverick

Tom Cruise was Hollywood's latest heartthrob—but he'd skipped town. After *Risky Business*, the twenty-two-year-old actor took a quick second bow with *All the Right Moves* (1983), then decamped to London to frolic in the woods. He was filming *Legend* (1985), directed by Ridley Scott, the British visionary who had just directed *Alien* (1979) and *Blade Runner* (1982), two history-making science fiction films. *Legend* was Ridley's fantasy opus, and Tom Cruise was his muse—or, really, his prop. Cruise spent nearly a year stuck in England, a victim of both ambition and bad luck. The capper was a huge fire that incinerated the film's indoor forest soundstage just ten days before the set was wrapped, requiring a panicked rebuild.

Like *Losin' It*, the over-budget fairy tale taught Cruise a lesson in the projects he needed to reject. "After that, I wanted to be careful about getting involved in a kind of epic production again," said Cruise. Worse, even though his impish, tree-dwelling Jack o' the Green was the film's supposed star, it wasn't a star-defining role. Cruise had to fight to stay visible in a film crowded with elves and dwarfs and Tim Curry's twelve-foot-tall Lord of Darkness. Admitted Cruise, "I don't think Ridley Scott necessarily needed me to do the movie. It could have been anyone in that part."[59]

The upside, if there was one, was that Cruise had an excuse to regroup and map out his career a whole ocean away from the teenybopper fame he wanted to avoid. (As Brits like *Peeping Tom* [1960] director Michael Powell sniffed, "Nobody would notice a boy with that little experience anywhere in Europe."[60]) But in Hollywood, Cruise was very much on the minds of Jerry Bruckheimer and Don Simpson, two hot-shot producers who drove matching black Ferraris and had just made their names with two simultaneous hits, *Flashdance* (1983) and *Beverly Hills Cop* (1984). Bruckheimer and Simpson read an article about risk-taking pilots in the Navy's flight school in Miramar and thrilled to the box office potential of a flag-waving flick about high-flying hunks. And they knew exactly who they wanted to star as daredevil pilot Pete "Maverick" Mitchell: Tom Cruise.

"Before we had a script, we went down to Miramar and met the pilots," said Simpson. "They look like Tom Cruise and act like Tom Cruise. They have the same bravado and yet innocence."[61] Cruise's résumé had no adult roles and only one starring hit. Yet Simpson and Bruckheimer weren't nervous—with *Flashdance*, they'd already proven they could cast an unknown like Jennifer Beals and still make a mint. Added Simpson, "He was the first person considered for this film, so we didn't get involved with going after anyone else."[62]

As for their direction, the producing duo had another unusual choice. Director Tony Scott's most recent film was the 1983 glossy vampire flop *The Hunger*, starring David Bowie. "I was on the bottom of the ladder,"[63] said Scott, but he'd shot a TV ad where a Saab raced a jet and the slick spot sold Bruckheimer and Simpson.

Tony Scott wasn't immediately onboard. He saw *Top Gun* as a dark *Apocalypse Now* (1979) for the Reagan Era. To try to align himself with the producers' vision, he flipped through a book of Bruce Weber photographs that included a shot where two Navy men posed with a classic car. Suddenly, the film clicked into focus. "They were good-looking, clean-cut, red-white-and-blue all-American boys," said Tony. "What I saw in their eyes embodied the characters that I wanted to portray in *Top Gun*." He, too, seized upon the young actor who had just shot *Legend* with his older brother Ridley. "One looked like Tom Cruise with a military haircut. That one picture made it kick in for me."[64]

Top Gun had its concept, its director, and its star. But there was one problem: Tom Cruise wouldn't say yes. "He thought it was *Flashdance* in the sky," recalled Simpson's then-assistant.[65] Cruise hated the script. Even Bruckheimer and Simpson hated the script. In the first draft turned in by Jim Cash and Jack Epps Jr., the crucial girlfriend role was written as a bimbo gymnast, and the fighting flight scenes felt jingoistic. Though Cruise liked the core idea of the film, he wasn't willing to risk his reputation on a disposable popcorn flick.

"If you look at *Top Gun*, you'd think even from the script that it has very good commercial potential. But *Top Gun* could have totally gone the other way," noted Cruise. "It's got to be a roller coaster ride, and it could have been a

Tony Scott and Tom Cruise
on the set of *Top Gun* (1986).

Opposite: Kelly McGillis plays
the hero's girl, a character
upgraded from a gymnast
to an astrophysicist.

kiddie ride."[66] Yet the concept stuck with him. "There wasn't a lot of script there, wasn't a lot of character. But it was gonna be different, and it was exciting for me to be part of that."[67] He offered Bruckheimer and Simpson an unusual deal: let *him* improve the script. If the final draft worked, he'd say yes. If not, he'd walk away. It was a bold proposition for a still-inexperienced actor—and a big gamble. Cruise risked investing time in a project that could have collapsed. However, if it worked, going forward he could push for the control to shape his own onscreen image. "I think they were kind of taken aback at first, but after coming off *Legend*, I just wanted to make sure that everything was gonna go the way we talked about it," explained Cruise.[68] Apprehensive but impressed, Simpson thought, "Wow, this guy had long distance savvy."[69]

The deal was odd to everyone except Tom Cruise. "It's always seemed natural to me to be involved." He shrugged. "I don't like to be at the mercy of scripts already written."[70] Describing his creative process, Cruise said, "When I first read a script, I just write down my first impressions—instinctive things on how I feel. I then put that piece of paper aside because once you read a script, you'll never get those exact feelings again." The trickiest part is balancing his innate drive while still seeing the script through the audience's fresh eyes. "You can be overworking something. You don't want to make yourself nuts."[71]

A Movie About Excellence

Miramar Naval Air Station was just two hours south of Los Angeles, so Cruise spent two months driving back and forth to earn the pilots' trust. He quickly realized what he didn't want in *Top Gun*: war. Groaned an adviser, "He wanted to make a movie about excellence. We wanted to make a movie about killing people."[72] Cruise refused to play an enlisted brute—he'd already done that in *Taps*. He wanted to play an athlete. His first flight in a mach-speed F-14 had left a physical impression. First, Cruise threw up. Then, as he described, "Your body contorts, your muscles get sore, and the straining forces blood from your brain. You grab your legs and your ass and grunt as the sweat pours over you."[73]

"He wanted to make this look like a sporting event," said Cruise's naval adviser Pete Pettigrew, "not about warmongering but about competition and excellence."[74] Excellence was fine. But the Navy wasn't happy with the fictional carrot-on-a-stick chase for a Top Gun trophy, or the topless locker room scenes. At Miramar, pilots were compatriots, not rivals who stripped off their shirts and sneered at each other between flights.

Simpson demanded the sexy towel-clad moments for the female audience. "Look, we're paying one million bucks to get [Cruise]," Simpson said to Pettigrew. "We need to see some flesh."[75] Again, the star and the filmmakers

Top Gun was the top-grossing flick of 1986 and the blockbuster that canonized Tom Cruise. But its effect on American culture didn't end there. That July—just two months after the film hit theaters—Navy recruitment officers reported that 90 per cent of all new applicants had seen *Top Gun*. That fall, Miramar celebrated a huge upsurge in tourism as goggle-eyed girls flocked to the local bars hoping to hook their own hunky fighter pilot.

Just as some critics had feared, Cruise had made the military cool. One year later, the Air Force begged Congress to pay $7.4 million for hip leather bomber jackets so their branch could keep pace with the spike in Navy enlistment—the same month, Soviet leader Mikhail Gorbachev visited Washington, D.C., and requested that a 35 mm print of *Top Gun* be delivered to his embassy. ("I didn't send it for propaganda purposes," insisted MPAA head Jack Valenti.[b])

But *Top Gun*'s repercussions weren't all fun and foreign relations. In 1991, Naval officers were accused of sexually assaulting eighty-three women at their annual Tailhook convention in Las Vegas. Who was to blame? Take a guess. "Prior to 1985, the only thing that happened at Tailhook was damage to the hotel," grumbled retired Navy aviator Nick Criss to the *Los Angeles Times*. "Suddenly, we were the superstars of the known world. Women were coming out of the woodwork and every one of them wanted to date a Navy aviator. We began seeing all these junior officers, little Tom Cruises, running around in their flight suits. They honestly believed the Navy was like the movie. I think to some extent, the Navy itself started behaving like it was the movie." Added Tailhook spokesman Steve Millikin, "All this Tom Cruise stuff crystallized into a message. Unfortunately, the wrong message."[c]

Opposite: When Maverick
Met Charlie... The bar scene
in Miramar.

Following pages: Goose
(Anthony Edwards) and
Maverick (Tom Cruise)
at the helm of their F-14.

disagreed. Cruise wanted to be seen as a serious actor, the producers wanted beefcake, and their director was caught in the middle. The young actor had a shrewd solution. He'd film the pinup scenes, but forbade on-set cameras from snapping stills, banning photographers outright during the oiled-up volleyball match. Further, he insisted on approval rights over all publicity shots released to the press. Cruise's pecs could only been seen onscreen. In print—the only place of permanence at the time—the image-conscious Cruise signed off only on shots that promoted his all-American brand: in a uniform, on a motorcycle, or in front of the flag.

On set, Tom Cruise started his days before dawn. (As Brickman had grumbled, so did Bruckheimer about how Cruise "would call me at 4 am about lines he wanted to make better."[76]) During the *Top Gun* shoot, he "functioned as much as a filmmaker as the star," observed *Newsweek*.[77] He'd brainstorm scenes for the other actors and spent his Sundays organizing meetings with the cast and crew to go over the week's schedule. To understand the rigors of being a Top Gun pilot, Cruise took classes in water survival and aviation physiology, and earned his flight certification. During the four days Cruise spent on the aircraft carrier USS *Enterprise*, he brought his own camera to record the activity on the flight deck. When the round-the-clock military schedule kept planes landing over his head until one o'clock in the morning, he simply gave up on rest and napped in the makeup chair between takes.

Cruise flew until he overcame his nausea. During one flight, he broke the sound barrier and then plummeted nose-down from 10,000 feet to 1,500 for kicks. "Good times," laughed Cruise. The preparation proved valuable when Scott strapped cameras around the F-14's backseat and told the pilots to take his actors soaring. Instead of great action shots, he got close-ups of Cruise's costars' vomit. Their reels were unusable. "Stuff is splattering all over the camera lens," joked Scott. But Cruise's shots made it into the film. "He was brilliant in the cockpit because he'd been in there before and knew what to do."[78]

Cruise's work ethic earned him the respect of the real Navy pilots. "He looked like a pilot, studied like a pilot, and sometimes even partied like a pilot," said an actual Top Gun.[79] His adviser, Pettigrew, went one step further: "He could easily have walked into Top Gun as a student or instructor. He's got that competitive personality."[80] But while Cruise bonded with his onscreen best friend Anthony Edwards—the usually-in-control twenty-three-year-old even drunkenly vomited in Edwards's BMW—when it came to establishing Maverick's estranged relationship with the other pilots, he cribbed from Francis Ford Coppola. During the *Outsiders* shoot, Coppola forced the downtrodden Greasers to stay at a dirty motel while his posh Socs slept in luxury. On camera, the

resentment was combustible. During *Top Gun*, Cruise did the same. He asked to stay in a separate building and strictly avoided Val Kilmer, who played Maverick's main nemesis, Iceman, a by-the-books pilot who considers his rival to be a dangerous thrill-seeker.

"Val and Tom never hung out together because they were these young, intense actors and they didn't want to cloud their relationship off-screen," said Scott. Cruise also avoided his character's on-again, off-again love interest, Kelly McGillis, to give their tentative romance extra awkward frisson. "The only times Val and Tom and Kelly came together was when they were onscreen," added Scott. "He was very conscientious."[81]

An Act Within an Act

The *Top Gun* cast and crew could attest to Cruise's behind-the-scenes sweat. But the actor was about to get a tough lesson in public perception. Like Tony Scott and his initial vision for *Top Gun*, critics in May of 1986 had their military fictions shaped by probing, cynical post-Vietnam films like *The Deer Hunter* (1978), *Apocalypse Now*, and even Cruise's own *Taps*. Despite the preproduction efforts by Cruise and the filmmakers to tamp down the violence in the original script, critics weren't warm to a flick that was cheerfully promilitary.

"The press shredded it, the press hated it," said Scott.[82] Reviews of *Top Gun* veered from hostile to condescending. Wrote *L.A. Style*, "This hyped-up recruiting poster for World War III needs no help from me,"[83] while those who thrilled to its wild visuals and old-fashioned eagerness-to-please stressed that they enjoyed its pleasures reluctantly. "*Top Gun* is a truly absurd movie, yet I enjoyed it almost as much as the 8-year-old boy within me had anticipated,"[84] was the *New York Times'* Vincent Canby's backhanded compliment, while the *LA Weekly*'s John Powers amusingly threw his hands up all together and listed nine reasons why he liked *Top Gun* paired with nine reasons why it pained him to admit it.[85]

However, the critical reaction to Cruise himself was curiously indifferent. A few personalized a remark he borrowed from one of his Top Gun instructors: "There are only four jobs in the world worth having: an actor, a rock star, a jet fighter pilot and President."[86] Sniffed the *Village Voice*'s J. Hoberman, "So much for gunrunning, ghostbusting and movie reviewing."[87] Many critics simply wrote him off altogether. "To say that the F-14 Tomcat is the real star of *Top Gun* would not be an overstatement,"[88] wrote *Film Journal* dismissively, while other critics merely mentioned Cruise's name in the plot description but saved their compliments for "true" talents like McGillis, who had just scored a Best Actress Golden Globe nomination for playing an Amish widow in *Witness* (1985). Even the critics who

complimented Cruise's performance did so for qualities that were out of his control—his eyes, his body, his "hawkish, slightly predatory look"[89]—as though the character's strengths were merely a by-product of smart casting.

Cruise craved respect for his craft. Instead, he was reduced to body parts. "Cruise combines the piercing blue eyes of Paul Newman with Nicholson's killer smile"[90] was a half-compliment in the *Washington Post* while the *New York Times* grumbled that he "brings little but a good build."[91] The *LA Times* even ran a feature where they counted up his facial expressions ("38 grins and 49 outright smiles with teeth flashing"[92]), and *Glamour* dithered, "In close-ups, the audience becomes intimate with the actor's major white teeth (the line dividing the two front ones is slightly off-center), and the muscle in his jaw which pulsates in emotional moments."[93]

These reactions weren't just superficial—they were blind. Not only did critics dismiss Cruise's performance, they missed altogether that it was a performance of a performance. Tom Cruise's Maverick acts cocky, but the cockiness is clearly an act. His brashness is overcompensation for his need to redeem his family's name after his father's plane disappeared over Vietnam, a personally-felt complication Cruise added during his two-month rewrite. ("Obviously, my father wasn't a fighter pilot and he didn't die a hero, but I think a lot of the gut-level, emotional stuff—the love of the father and the conflict in that—is in there."[94]) He's emotionally injured, a wounded soldier surrounded by fellow gladiators, and to keep from being torn apart or written off as a failure, he self-inflates with swagger. Studying Cruise, it's clear that Maverick is all bluster—he's phony for two-thirds of the film—but critics bought Cruise's act, to his own detriment.

Highway to the Danger Zone

In the air, Maverick does what he wants. But on the ground, he's caged. He opens the film in flight, zooming upside-down above an enemy plane to give them the finger. The scene establishes him as rebellious, but in the very next scene, he's on land—or, technically, an aircraft carrier—and that image is corrected. Maverick is no over-the-top loudmouth but a lower status military man forced to stay quiet while being upbraided by his commanding officer. He's not allowed to smile—he's barely allowed to blink—and Cruise carries himself with the stiff posture of someone who knows he can express himself only alone on his motorcycle or 10,000 feet high in a plane. The only reaction Cruise affords the character is a furtive jaw clench when his commander, Stinger (James Tolkan), mentions his dad.

Everything Maverick does is a performance. *Top Gun* is more about psychological warfare than the actual battlefield. In Miramar, when he first meets Iceman, Hollywood, and the rest of his rivals for the Top Gun trophy, his fearlessness is an act designed to convince everyone, including himself, that he's the best pilot before they even take flight. Cruise's body language isn't natural confidence; it's over-the-top artificial, from his calculated smile to the forced casualness of how he twirls his pencil. He's the only one smiling as Viper (Tom Skerritt) lectures the class on being the best of the best, and he drops the act only when Iceman shoots him a grin that's even bigger and phonier.

Cruise doesn't oversell Maverick's feigned confidence. Instead of sticking out his chest and bellowing, Maverick is soft-spoken. When Viper asks if he'll win the Top Gun trophy, Cruise doesn't bark "Yes, sir!" but instead meets the officer's gaze and says the words calmly in a voice that's quiet, candid, and convincing.

Only Anthony Edwards's Goose is allowed to see the real Maverick, and even then only when they're alone. In public, their relationship is a tag-team act. At the bar on the first night in Miramar, Edwards doubles over with fake guffaws when Iceman and Hollywood call him "Mother Goose." A minute later, when Goose dares him to seduce Charlie (Kelly McGillis), Maverick doesn't risk the emotional peril of being himself. Instead, he grabs a microphone and sings "You've Lost That Lovin' Feelin'"—a stunt guaranteed to burnish his reputation among the guys as a risk-taker even if he fails at his mission. And Cruise, an excellent singer, deliberately makes Maverick croon off-key. Not only does his choice make Maverick more vulnerable and endearing, it proves his character isn't naturally slick—a smoother man wouldn't sing if he warbled. The crowd buys his confidence, but Maverick knows the truth. When Charlie asks if he thinks his routine was a success, he jokes, "Tell you tomorrow," with a forced laugh that admits this is a game he always figured he'd lose.

Back in the locker room, Iceman publicly corners Maverick to accuse him of unsafe flying. Again, Cruise does the unexpected. Most actors would have read the line, "That's right, Iceman. I am dangerous," as reactionary anger. Cruise gives the words a self-aware showiness with hyperenunciation and an odd speech pattern. "That's *right*. Ice. Man. I *am* dangerous," he purrs, stroking Iceman's shoulder. There's nothing natural in his response—Maverick is imitating the tough guys he's seen in movies. Cruise is acting at acting, and critics who found Maverick callow missed the difference. And the point.

Cruise doesn't let Maverick get real until he's off the base, away from the boys, and alone with McGillis's Charlie. Only then does Maverick relax, even though Cruise's intense eye contact practically burns through the screen as he visibly absorbs all the information he can to glean how their date is going. We can even see in his face

Opposite, top: A simmering rivalry between Maverick and Iceman (Val Kilmer).

Opposite, bottom: Maverick and Goose stand to attention as their superior (Tom Skerritt) tears into them.

the moment he decides to call Charlie's bluff that they're merely buddies by calculatedly noting she's been too distracted by him to uncork the wine. Their true dynamic established, Maverick opens up about his mother's love of Motown, his father's mysterious disappearance, and his own need to succeed. But as important is Cruise's body language. He stops standing at attention and simply relaxes. It's only here that Charlie—and the audience—is finally allowed to truly warm to him, and while Cruise's grin is still big, it's ditched the forced, at-attention sharpness.

Top Gun is fascinated with the divide between private life and public performance. Because of their instructor/student dynamic, Charlie insists on hiding their love affair. On the base, she flagrantly turns down his dates and insults his attack strategies, then furtively passes notes and chases him down after class. Sharing an elevator with a fellow officer, they stand on opposite sides of the car like strangers. They're only at ease when the third wheel leaves and they can halt the machine between floors to steal a moment alone. When Charlie admits her harsh attacks on Maverick's flying were a ruse to hide her love, Cruise's face flickers with warring emotions. Is his ego stroked or bruised? He gives up and moves in for their first kiss.

Maverick's happiness is temporary. *Top Gun* is about striving, not success. Goose's death in an ejection-seat accident topples Maverick's

confidence. Now, he can't convince even himself that he's the best. He hasn't just lost his cockiness—he's lost his ability to simulate cockiness, and Cruise physically shuts Maverick down. Before the crash, Cruise looked confidently at the world. In his first scene after Goose's accident, Maverick stares at himself in the mirror, and it's practically the last facial contact he'll hold for the last third of the film. Post-crash, he can't meet anyone's eyes. The smile is gone; the bluster is gone. All that Cruise keeps is Maverick's practiced military posture, which he holds when the Naval court decides whether to allow him back in the air. Like his earlier scenes with his superiors, he stands at attention. But though the poses look outwardly the same, instead of his former hyperalertness, Cruise lets Maverick's gaze drift past the proceedings. His silent inattention speaks volumes: he's so shaken up by death that he can't even care if he loses the right to fly.

True to form, Maverick keeps his sadness buried within, which forces Cruise to carry the weight of feelings his character can't express. In his heaviest scene, he attempts to comfort Goose's widow, played by new starlet Meg Ryan. The script called for Cruise to enter her room clutching a box of Goose's belongings. But when the cameras rolled, Cruise realized that Maverick wouldn't have the bravery to cross the doorway. Instead, he stood next to the entrance and froze, the actor realizing that his character was unable to

play the part of the strong soldier. He asked Scott if they could end the shot at the doorframe instead.

"I think it's something he took from a moment that he had with his family, death in his family, where he couldn't come to terms with going through that door to face the family," mused Scott. "He went for the door and couldn't get out. He closed the door again. I thought it was a really great moment."[95]

Tellingly, we never see Maverick find the courage to walk through the door. Scott cuts to Cruise already inside the room. We're expecting him to soothe Ryan's young widow, but he can't even do that. Because of her close relationship with her husband's wingman, she knows how to interpret Maverick's stiffness. Instead of taking offense, she gives him a hug. Over her shoulder, Cruise's face is a silent storm. He can't let Maverick cry, but he's got to show us the simmering sadness as he stoically tenses his jaw and breathes.

Not *Just* a Movie Star

Pauline Kael ridiculed Charlie's breakup line to Maverick: "When I first met you, you were larger than life." (She snickered that the strapping, forced-to-slouch McGillis would say that about "such a Nautilized, dinky thing."[96]) But Cruise's physicality proves those words true. Maverick's implosion showcases the contrast between Cruise's first act posturing and his third act deflation. Somewhere in the middle—in his mellow moments with Goose and Charlie—are the only times Maverick is himself. A close read of Cruise's performance shows how skillfully he created Maverick's layers and range. Yet *Variety* still wrote off his role as "one-note grinning."[97] Bruckheimer and Simpson's monster hit swaggered into the summer of '86 with so much bombast that people didn't look beyond its slick surface. *Top Gun* was a popcorn movie starring a teen heartthrob—why would it bother having craft? Ironically, though the film made Tom Cruise a household name and gave him behind-the-scenes clout, it risked derailing his serious ambitions.

"People say, 'Oh, you were just a movie star in that role,'" Cruise complained. "But I always thought I was an actor playing a movie star in that role."[98] Perhaps he played the role too well. At the end of 1986, *Top Gun* was the highest-grossing film of the year and Cruise was king of the blockbusters. Even when Simpson and Bruckheimer offered to quintuple his salary, he turned down *Top Gun 2*. "I knew there was no room for a sequel," said Cruise. "That time had passed."[99]

At an age where his high-school friends were just graduating college, Cruise was rejecting a fortune. Where did he get the courage? Something else had happened during the filming of *Top Gun*. "In the middle of the movie, I got a call, and I was offered this Paul Newman–Martin Scorsese picture," said Cruise. "And I read it and immediately said, 'Yeah. Can't wait.' I couldn't believe that this was happening to me. And I knew then that *Top Gun* wasn't the only kind of movie that I would be able to make."[100]

The movie star wanted to be an actor. Convincing the critics to agree would require an even greater performance.

Maverick is unable to comfort his best friend's widow, played by Meg Ryan in one of her first roles.

3

Ron Kovic

Born on the Fourth of July (1989)
Oliver Stone

"I wanna get out of this fucking body I'm in."
—Ron Kovic

"Tom is at a disadvantage," declared director Barry Levinson. "He's got a pretty face, so his abilities are underestimated. And he's not working a rebel image, which is associated with being a good actor."[101] Cruise was coming to the same conclusion. "I started to realize that what the public and the critics see—like whether they take me seriously—reflects what they perceive as what's right for me," he recognized.[102] Time to expand their perception beyond the cocky, callow, charismatic winner. Most young, wildly popular stars—not that his contemporaries were *as* popular—would've followed *Top Gun* with another megawatt, megasalary starring role to solidify their position in the big leagues. Not Cruise. Instead, he made a strategic sidestep: he signed on to play second fiddle to Paul Newman in *The Color of Money* (1986) and Dustin Hoffman in *Rain Man.*

"I don't have any ego about whose movie it is," Cruise explained.[103] In *The Color of Money*, Cruise played a brash, hotshot pool player struggling under the guidance of Paul Newman's Fast Eddie Felson, a reprise of his snooker swindler in 1961's *The Hustler.* In *Rain Man*, Cruise played a brash, hotshot car salesman struggling to poach his autistic older brother Raymond's inheritance. Newman won the Best Actor Oscar for *Color of Money* in 1987. Hoffman won the Best Actor Oscar for *Rain Man* in 1989. Neither Academy Award ceremony nominated Tom Cruise. No matter—the association was enough.

Cruise cannily tried to trade cash for prestige, but even so he earned more than he expected. Financially, both films were box office successes way beyond their backers' imaginations. *The Color of Money* made more than Scorsese's two biggest previous hits, *Raging Bull* (1980) and *Taxi Driver* (1976), combined, and *Rain Man* astonished the industry when this R-rated autism drama became the number one hit of 1988. Cruise's clout was beyond doubt. For him, however, the real prize was the opportunity to study the craft of two acting legends.

"He has Newman's sincerity and Hoffman's ability to mime," wrote *Rolling Stone.* Yet Cruise wanted to learn, not just imitate. Asked if Newman and Hoffman were his mentors, Cruise replied, "Absolutely right, that's how I felt."[104] From the two very different greats, the young actor picked up separate acting lessons. Of Hoffman, to whom Roger Ebert compared him in his review of *Risky Business*, Cruise noted, "I've watched the way he achieves almost a lyrical pace to his work."[105] Handsome Newman, however, was closer to Cruise's own Hollywood niche. Both specialized in charmers with surprising depth, and for good and ill, their relationship framed the next several years of Cruise's career. (Newman hooked Cruise on race car driving, leading directly to 1990's poorly received *Days of Thunder.*)

"Look at Newman, look at what this man has created as an actor and a human being," gushed Cruise.[106] A pretty boy who'd earned an Oscar nomination just four years after his Hollywood debut, Newman had steadily, patiently stayed relevant and marketable even as the industry transitioned from the dramatic fifties to the rebellious sixties and seventies to the slick eighties—a longevity Cruise was determined to forge. To critics who dismissed his performances as fluff, he pointed to Newman as a rebuttal. "If that's what people think of me, then I take it as a compliment. The whole goal is not to see the actor working," said Cruise. "Talk about making it look easy—you can't catch Newman acting."[107] Added Cruise, "If all I've done seems easy to people, you've got to remember you can only work with the roles that are made available to you. What people have seen so far with me is a young actor at the beginning of his career. I know that the films have been very successful, but it's still just the beginning for me."[108] *The Color of Money* and *Rain Man* had given him prestige, but no award nominations—and he was in peril of being typecast as a money-grubbing hotshot. Enter Oliver Stone with exactly the challenge Cruise needed.

"Tom Understands"

Oliver Stone had spent a decade trying to make *Born on the Fourth of July*, the biopic of paraplegic Vietnam veteran Ron Kovic. In 1977, he'd come close, even announcing Al Pacino

Tom Cruise plays a paraplegic Vietnam vet in Oliver Stone's *Born on the Fourth of July* (1989).

as the lead. After Pacino ditched the project to shoot …*And Justice For All* (1979), financing collapsed and Stone reluctantly shelved the film. But in 1986, the same year Cruise soared high as Maverick, Stone released *Top Gun*'s dark counterpart, *Platoon*. When *Platoon* won four Oscars, Stone seized the opportunity to shoot his dream project. Pacino was too old and "a schmuck," grumbled Stone,[109] so he seized upon the idea of casting his inverse—an actor who represented the eighties the way Pacino represented the seventies. He looked to the star of *Platoon*'s competition: Tom Cruise.

"I saw this kid who has everything. And I wondered what would happen if tragedy strikes, if fortune denies him […]," mused Stone. "I thought it was an interesting proposition: what would happen to Tom Cruise if something goes wrong?"[110] To *Time* magazine, Stone's explanation was even sharper. "He's a kid off a Wheaties box. I wanted to yank the kid off the box and mess with his image—take him to the dark side."[111]

The suits were onboard. "Tom Cruise is America's all-American boy. The film's journey is more powerful when it's made by the Maverick from *Top Gun*," said Universal head Tom Pollock. "It's not only Ron who goes through this wrenching story, it is Tom Cruise, our perception of Tom Cruise."[112] The financial bonus didn't hurt. "Tom Cruise was an interesting choice, but not a brave one," added *Born on the Fourth of July*'s producer Martin Bregman. "Given his popularity with the youth audience, Cruise could do Tom Pollock's Bar Mitzvah picture and it would do well commercially."[113]

Cruise didn't hesitate. He read just twenty pages of the script before calling Paula Wagner, who also represented Oliver Stone, and insisting they make the movie. Stone's financing problems were over. In fact, adding Cruise's name to the poster nearly doubled the initial budget. Even so, Cruise agreed to a salary cut—his real reward would be the artistic credibility. And unlike Pacino, Cruise was committed. "Believe me, we're going to make this movie," he assured Stone. "I'm not going anywhere."[114] But if the film was going to be any good, one more person had to agree: Ron Kovic.

"I wondered if he had the depth to portray me," admitted the wheelchair-bound veteran, who lost control of his body below his chest after taking a bullet in the spine in Vietnam's demilitarized zone. For once, Cruise's superficial pinup image was an advantage. "He's so full of life. He's so sure. He's so representative of America before the war," said Kovic. "He's about to go through this hell, and he doesn't even know it."[115] Stone drove Cruise over to Kovic's house for an introduction, and the two men spent an afternoon talking over Kovic's photos, books, and home movies.

"I felt an instant rapport with him that I never experienced with Pacino," said Kovic. After several hours, Kovic began to cry. "Oliver asked if I was OK," he recalled. Kovic replied, "'Tom understands, he really understands.'"[116] Still, the press sharpened their sabers. When Cruise was announced, one magazine sniffed that the teen idol in a wheelchair was miscasting as terrible as "if his crony Sean Penn were to take the lead in *Gandhi II*."[117] But Kovic and Cruise were more alike than critics realized. Kovic, as the title implies, was born on the fourth of July. Cruise was born on the third. Both men were raised as working-class Catholics surrounded by sisters. Both wrestled in high school, skipped out of higher education, and believed they could succeed at anything if they gave it their all. "Like Ron, too, Tom is wound real tight," said Stone, "and what's wrong with that?"[118] Their main difference was luck. Ron enlisted as a Marine to prove his worth and became paralyzed. Cruise, however, had seen his gambles pay off again and again.

"Cruise was cocky, sure he could handle everything," said Stone. "But I wasn't so sure. I saw he'd bitten off a lot—more than he'd thought."[119] Stone decided to shoot the film in continuity as much as the schedule allowed so Cruise could simulate Kovic's journey from shallow to shattered to the patron saint of wounded soldiers. For his part, Cruise was determined to understand paralysis. Kovic introduced him to other handicapped men, and joked to the press that Cruise learned how to do a wheelie in thirty seconds. During one of the rare interviews he agreed to during production, Cruise arrived at a crowded mall in a wheelchair and observed the unawares journalist until the writer was about to leave. Cruise finally rolled over and said, "Guess it's working."[120]

Stone wanted to take Cruise's Method acting further. He discovered a drug that would actually freeze Cruise's legs for two days at a time. "I put a lot of pressure on Tom, maybe too much," said Stone. "Then the insurance company—the killer of all experience—said no because there was a slight chance that Tom would have ended up permanently paralyzed. But the point is, he was willing to do it."[121]

Dodging the stunt was a blessing. Cruise didn't need to be drugged, and he didn't need critics questioning whether he did need to be drugged—it would have been perceived as a literal crutch. Plus, at its core *Born on the Fourth of July* isn't about paralysis. It's about a veteran duped into fighting a hopeless and unpopular war, then returning home to fight a new enemy: his disengaged family, friends, and country, even himself. Paralyzed or not, it was a difficult shoot. As tensions escalated in Kovic's biography, tensions escalated on the set. After a tough day, Cruise chased down Kovic during the

Ron Kovic loses his big match. He will try to earn back the town's respect by enlisting in the army.

Following pages: Ron Kovic and his high school buddies: Timmy (Frank Whaley), Joey (Richard Panebianco), Tommy (Rob Camilletti), Steve (Jerry Levine), and Billy (Stephen Baldwin, obscured).

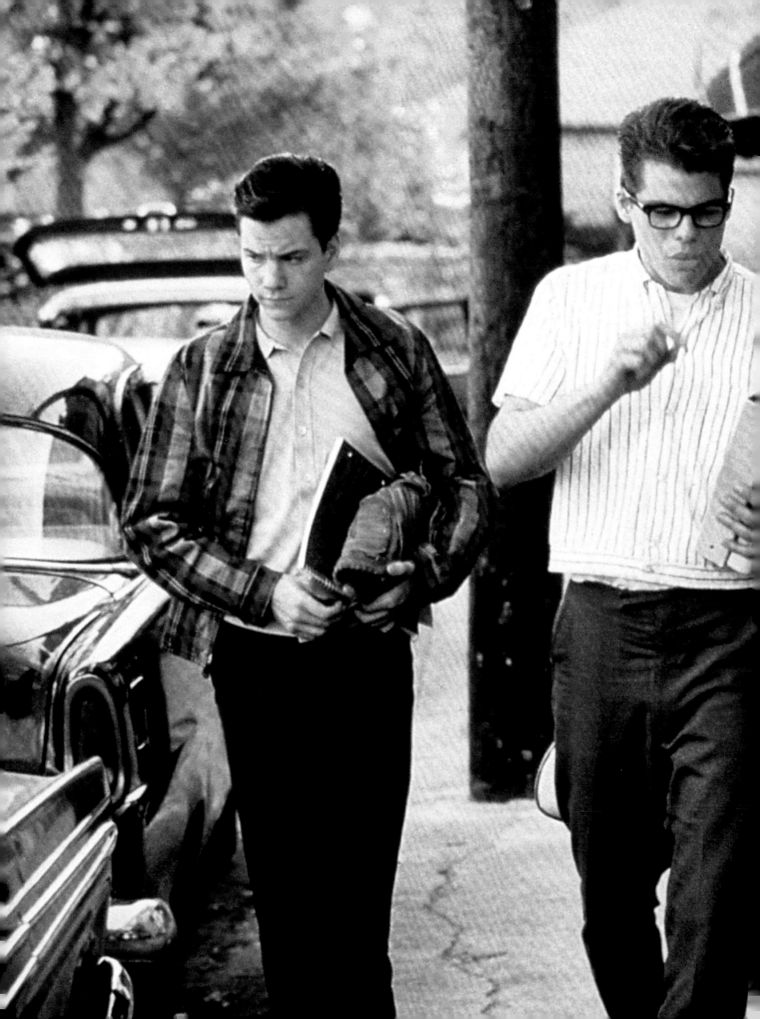

drive home. "Cruise rolled down the window of his jeep he was driving and yelled, 'Why does your life have to be so difficult, so challenging? This is very difficult for me,'" recalled Kovic. "We cursed and shouted and laughed back and forth and all the frustration came out. I began to realize that I wasn't alone, that Tom was paying a price for this film too."[122]

Cruise and the studio had their disagreements, too. Cruise had fought—and won—the right to suppress his beefcake shots from *Top Gun*. Now he wanted to do the opposite: flood the press with photos of himself in a wheelchair to kick-start his image-changing campaign. Universal refused, fearful of turning off the audience who wanted to see Cruise the hero. This time, the actor lost. He'd have to wait for *Born on the Fourth of July*'s release and let his performance make the case.

Two Wars

Born on the Fourth of July tells the story of a not-too-bright blue-collar kid who wants to do right by the values of the conservative 1950s: work hard, defend democracy, marry a good woman, make America proud. He fails, and then his country fails him. Tom Cruise plays Kovic from seventeen to thirty, the years in which Kovic enlists in Vietnam, commits atrocities, becomes paralyzed, and struggles with his slow recognition that he's sacrificed his body for a government and its citizens who don't want to be reminded of what he and his war represent. It's a painful arc that starts at ignorance, bottoms out in misery, and ends in righteous anger as the veteran rails against war at the 1976 Democratic National Convention.

Ron Kovic is a striver, not a thinker. Forget Maverick—he's pure obedience. In an early montage, Cruise grimly and blankly obeys his wrestling coach's orders to do push-ups, climb ropes, and run in the snow. But for Kovic—unlike Cruise—hard work isn't enough. He loses the big match, and before the referee even calls it, Cruise's face collapses into anguish. He already knows he's lost the town's respect—and trying to earn it back will cost him everything.

Kovic's faith in his country's values is blind, and it's visible in Cruise's face. His eyes have lost *Top Gun*'s laser focus, and his boyish whisper, last heard in Joel Goodsen, parrots ideas about communism and war that he's overheard on the television. Saddled with braces, he squeaks, "I'll die there if I have to," but he doesn't sound like he understands what those words mean. Alone, he prays to God about his confusion. But in public, Kovic is all bluster—and Cruise's subtle immaturity clues us in that Kovic, unlike Maverick, isn't clever enough to know it.

Kovic fights two wars: one in Vietnam and a second at home. In the Asia sequence, Stone cuts straight to Kovic's second tour, where Cruise's confident but dulled body language shows that Kovic is used to grenades. He gives orders, but also accepts them unthinkingly, even pretending to see enemy rifles at his commanding officer's insistence. In *Born*'s first wrenching scene, Kovic accidentally kills one of his own men during an ambush. Cruise scrambles to the corpse on his knees—Kovic's legs still work, but from this soul-shattering moment on, he's already emotionally crippled. Back at camp, he tries to confess. "I think I might have killed him," Cruise says weakly. He repeats the line three times, and each time his voice stiffens as though the truth is finally sinking in.

Cruise lets the guilt weigh on his face. His eyes become cold and narrowed, while his mind looks adrift. During the fateful attack that leaves him paralyzed, Cruise curses and screams, but with resignation, as though he's been waiting—even hoping—for death. When the bullet comes, Cruise's face isn't even pointed toward the enemy. He's looking over his shoulder, at though impatient to see what hell comes next. In the wailing emergency military transport carrier, he accepts his fate and doesn't cry. When a priest reads his late rites, he barely even blinks.

Compare Kovic in Vietnam to Kovic's fight for recognition in post-Vietnam America, an equally chaotic battlefield where policemen, flash-bang grenades, and poison gas terrify the protestors. Outside of the 1972 Republican National Convention in Miami, Kovic is now wholly present and in command. Using the military speech and bearing he honed in *Taps* and *Top Gun*, Cruise shows us the shift from boy soldier to civilian commander. He sits upright, stares clearly at the world, and strips the hesitation from his voice. When he barks, "Let's move!" his followers obey, just as he once obeyed his coach and commanding officers.

Kovic has lost the use of his legs, but the actor is finally in command of his character's eyes, arms, and mouth. Once failing and unfocused, now he masterfully uses all three: staring down the journalists, pushing himself taller in front of the news cameras, and screaming for attention when policemen try to drag him away. The Cruise persona—power, charisma, ambition—has finally merged with Kovic's life story. He's no longer conforming to people's expectations—he's saying what people don't want to hear.

Maturation wasn't easy. During the long, sad stretch in between, Cruise rides waves of conflicting emotions as Kovic attempts to make sense of his sacrifice. Like Cruise himself, Kovic is an optimist. In the early days of his injury at a rat-ridden veterans' hospital, he vows, "I'm walking out of here, guys—you'll see." Because this is Tom Cruise, the audience almost believes him. Crutching pridefully fast, he's the Maverick of the rec room. But *Born* isn't

54

"I'm walking out of here, guys—you'll see." Because this is Tom Cruise, the audience almost believes him.

Following pages: Back home with his brothers Jimmy (Jamie Talisman), Tommy (Josh Evans), and Jackie (Kevin Harvey Morse), his father (Raymond J. Barry) and his sister Patty (Samantha Larkin).

a typical Cruise movie: he falls, and his femur snaps. Fans collapsed. *Variety* reported that ten people fainted during the leg-breaking scene on opening weekend alone. Stone's droll response: "The sound of people sleeping would be more of a concern."[123]

Strapped facedown and staring at his own vomit, Cruise allows Kovic to release his frustrations. "I just want to be treated d-d-d-decent! *Decent!*" he yelps. In contrast to Cruise's stiff stillness in *Risky Business*, now when actually paralyzed, the actor lashes out with his limbs: he screams, he smashes, he throws cups and wails. His sobbing breakdown gives the next scene its quiet power. Home for the first time, wheelchair-bound Kovic acts the confident, returning hero who brags about his pull-up routine. The audience alone knows that the famous smile is a mask. "Everyone looks so good," he grins, and in return his family and neighbors parrot that he "looks good, looks good" to underscore that his reentrance into the community is entirely superficial.

Like Maverick, Kovic won't cop to his inner pain. He must live up to being an American soldier—once more, Cruise is performing at performing. So he lies, insisting at a Fourth of July rally that morale in Vietnam is high and America will win the war. On display at a parade, he smiles and waves—but when he flinches at exploding fireworks, Cruise's eyes show the trauma Kovic isn't ready to express.

Cruise allows Kovic to get honest only around a fellow soldier, his childhood friend Timmy (Frank Whaley). With Timmy, he smiles his first real postwar smile and even laughs a genuine laugh, albeit at the gallows humor of another friend killed by a flying tree. Still, when the men tentatively question Vietnam, Cruise looks away from the camera and numbs his voice as the words—like the ideas—come to him slowly. *Born* isn't about Kovic's triumph; it's about his painful path. This is merely his first step.

Kovic's struggle for truth swerves between two polarities: shallow patriotism and bitter cynicism. You can measure his mood by the length of his hair: military crop, hospital shag, slicked into a ponytail, or wild and crazy. When his locks get bigger, so does Cruise's performance. Politicized after seeing his childhood sweetheart (Kyra Sedgwick) battered by the cops, Kovic next appears long-haired and drunk in a billiards hall as he finally rages against Vietnam. But the forced cheer in Cruise's voice makes his opinions still sound immature. We're glad Kovic is angry, but Cruise won't let us applaud. Instead, he plays the scene like a grating drunk. Even wheelchair-bound, his physical anger is apparent: he paces, then flails his head injuriously on the dance floor. "I just wanna dance!" he yells. It's painful to see the former Joel Goodsen unable to cut loose.

Nothing Left to Give

In the second half of the film, Cruise can't keep silent. As Kovic rages against his broken body, Cruise savages his former screen image. Drunk in front of his onscreen parents, Cruise sarcastically snaps his *Taps* salute, mocks *Top Gun*'s militarism, and screams that he wants "a big fucking erect penis." ("For any man, the thought of losing his penis is frightening on so many levels," Cruise admitted to *Playboy*. "I could feel this script in my balls."[124]) But Cruise keeps us aware that Kovic isn't ready to destroy the system, at least not yet. Even as Cruise's mouth moves, his eyes are uncomprehending, his questions hitting him at the moment he says them aloud. He doesn't have answers as he crumbles to ask, "Who's going to love me, Dad?"

Like Cruise, Kovic was handsome. But the actor has to sell us on Kovic's clumsiness with women: he's too shy to seduce his high-school sweetheart, too injured and insecure to ask her for a second chance, and finally, too broken to enjoy his paid-for moments with a series of Mexican prostitutes. In his teen scenes, Cruise buries his charisma under awkward bravado. He pretends not to care about his high-school sweetheart until he does the only daring thing in his young life: surprise her at prom. When he returns from war, we can see his eagerness to impress her in his neat hair and the gleam in his eyes. Like Maverick, he even tries to woo her with a song. (Unlike Maverick, Cruise allows himself to sing in tune.) But he's so afraid of rejection, of risking the truth that she might not be able to love a man in a chair, that he pretends they're merely friends.

In conventional biopics, a good woman saves an injured man. Not here. Cruise decamps to an expat community of veterans and prostitutes in Mexico. In bed with a tender, but no-nonsense older woman—Cruise's third virginity-loss scene, third hooker scene, and second Mexican hooker scene—he nervously protests when she takes off his pants because he's afraid to disappoint her and himself. She accepts, and ignores, his fears. The scene is almost religious in its intensity: she kisses his forehead, nuzzles his chest, and after they make a version of love, Cruise starts to cry.

"It was a hard few days. Tom is very shy [...]," said Stone of the physically and emotionally naked shoot. "On one take, something happened inside him. Those tears come from someplace in Tom."[125] Kovic dares to love, but he's chosen the wrong woman. Quickly heartbroken, Cruise clicks back into his artificial cool, and we never see him act romantically vulnerable again. With the next hooker, he's closed-off and cold, a man who accepts—prematurely perhaps—that love isn't an option.

Now bitterly wise, Cruise stares flatly at the world. In a scene of Brechtian black comedy,

Kovic and fellow crippled vet Charlie (Willem Dafoe) bicker about who deserves to be more miserable while stranded in the Mexican desert. It's the film's lowest point, when even veterans can't comfort veterans, but Cruise adds agonizing humor. "Maybe I killed a whole bunch of babies, but I don't have to talk about it!" he shrieks, getting into a slap fight that ends with the two tumbling into the dust. The scene is sour and funny and completely dependent on Cruise tapping into his own raw exhaustion. "A crew member leaned over to me and whispered, 'He's doing it, he's doing it,'" recalled Kovic. "We all knew something special was happening, and that Tom Cruise was right in the middle of it…"[126]

"All I know is that I gave Oliver everything on this movie. I have nothing left to give, absolutely nothing left," said Cruise when the *Born* shoot finally wrapped.[127] "Tom gave the performance of his life, going to the ragged edge, at great risk to himself,"[128] declared Kovic, who presented Cruise with his own Bronze Star Medal, awarded for heroism in combat. He'd won Kovic's respect. Now for the critics.

The Real Thing

Cruise used his press tour to distance his new, serious image from the *Top Gun* heartthrob. He was well aware that the press delighted in the irony that the Maverick who boosted military enlistment was now about-facing. "Think of that: I am totally responsible for World War Three!" Cruise laughed to a reporter who pressed him about whether *Top Gun* had created a new generation of Ron Kovics. "*Top Gun* was just an amusement park ride, a fun film with a PG-13 rating that was not supposed to be reality. That's why I didn't go on and make *Top Gun* 2 and 3 and 4 and 5. That would have been irresponsible." Disavowing his biggest hit, he continued, "I didn't have anything riding on *Top Gun*. The fact is, I really want people to see *Born of the Fourth of July*,"[129] while to *Us* magazine, he was even more blunt: "*Top Gun* was a game. This is the real thing."[130]

Most bought Cruise's campaign. *Time* wrote, "Everything that was terrific in, say, *Top Gun*—the war, the sex, the male bonding—is found to be toxic here."[131] Others found this new, serious Cruise a touch pretentious. *Rolling Stone* couldn't resist a jab that he was now calling himself an "actor-artist," and then pressed him if his "traditional audience" would buy tickets to *Born*. "You're the type of person who stereotypes things," Cruise groaned. "I was never worried about giving up my looks or my body."[132] Yet *New York* magazine critic David Denby deftly merged Cruise's screen idol presence with the film's severity. "In the past, he has seemed callow, a failing he disguised

with cockiness. But Ron Kovic, who believed everything his parents and his country told him, was himself callow, and when Cruise shrieks in dismay, he sounds right."[133]

"He could always do *Top Gun II* and they'd come out in droves," argued Stone. "If he confined himself to those roles, though, his soul risked dying. This film gave him an enormous amount of self-respect."[134] It also risked draining Cruise of his youthful charisma. "A part of Tom has passed from youth to middle age," said Stone. Just as *Platoon* sucked something out of Sheen, it will be hard for Tom to go back to being innocent again. He'll always carry around Kovic."[135]

Two years after his internships with Dustin Hoffman and Paul Newman, Cruise's performance in *Born on the Fourth of July* earned him Best Actor nominations at both the Golden Globes and the Academy Awards. He won the Globe—his first trophy—but lost the Oscar to Daniel Day-Lewis for *My Left Foot* (1989), another wheelchair-bound role. Cruise had done painful, hard-won, unflattering work, but Day-Lewis outdid him by learning to write, type, and paint with his foot, and contorting himself so much that two of his vertebrae had to be realigned. While Cruise was content to act paralyzed, Day-Lewis refused to leave his chair during the entire production, forcing grumbling grips to carry him from set to set. Cruise's

handicapped performance in *Born* was more than a stunt—but even so, he'd been outstunted.

Still, to come in second to the man deemed the world's best actor was a compliment. But comparisons to Day-Lewis would soon become a curse Cruise couldn't shake.

Vanity Fair journalist Jesse Kornbluth spent a day with a wheelchair-bound Tom Cruise at the Galleria Mall in Dallas, Texas. Here's an excerpt from their afternoon, including Cruise's conversation with a handicapped child.

Cruise was in a fine mood as we turned back toward the skating rink to meet his cousin. We'd spent enough time together for me to forget that he was in a wheelchair, that the Tom Cruise I was seeing wasn't the Tom Cruise who wears the expensive Italian clothes in *Rain Man*....
Then we saw the kid in the wheelchair.
He was looking out over the skating rink. He couldn't have been more than nine. And his wheelchair wasn't something he'd borrowed for a movie. Cruise rolled right over to him. "Hey, man, what's your name?"
The boy told him.
"Some shopping center, huh?"
The boy agreed that the Galleria was something else. "Where are you from?"
Cruise had friends there. They talked about the Olympics, the restaurant where the boy and his family had eaten lunch, and the skating lessons the boy was watching. They haven't fallen over once, he reported.
"Well, you take care of yourself," Cruise said. He patted the boy's arm and we moved on.
Dead silence.
Doesn't it kill him that he can walk away from his wheelchair?
"Listen, you talk to people in wheelchairs, they don't want to see me in a chair," he said, less sharply than I might have. "And they don't want you to feel sorry for them. They work like hell to live and be alive; if they didn't want to be alive, they wouldn't be. But seeing a boy

in a wheelchair like that... it's not easy. It's not easy to go home and say, 'Hey, I'm getting it.'"
We'd gotten to the car. Cruise wrenched himself from the front seat. His legs, still limp, dangled out. With difficulty, he reached over and lifted them in, one at a time. "I have to practice my transfers," he said at the end of this long procedure. He settled back and made small talk, but he had filed that flaw in his character. I knew that he'd practice that move many more times. And that, long before he had to be filmed in a car, he'd have it right—because in the universe Tom Cruise now inhabits, even the defects have to be perfect. [d]

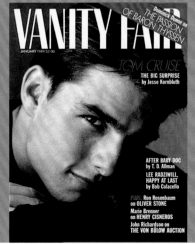

4

Lestat de Lioncourt

Interview with the Vampire: The Vampire Chronicles (1994)
Neil Jordan

"Evil is a point of view."
—Lestat de Lioncourt

When Warner Bros. began developing Anne Rice's *Interview with the Vampire*, Tom Cruise was a former teen idol continually battling his mainstream blockbuster status. Daniel Day-Lewis was a Shakespearean-trained thespian who stormed Hollywood with his credibility already cast in stone. Cruise had played soldiers and playboys, and learned to shoot pool, fly planes, race cars, and spin liquor bottles. Day-Lewis played gay men and Victorian snobs, and studied Czech, trained himself to hunt and trap, and even claimed to have been haunted by his father's ghost while performing *Hamlet* onstage at London's National Theatre. Yet three years after the two fiercely driven, wildly different actors fought for the 1990 Best Actor Oscar, Cruise and Day-Lewis were being compared again—and once more, Cruise was the underdog.

After seventeen years and countless screenplay drafts, Anne Rice's 1976 bestseller *Interview with the Vampire* was finally green-lit, thanks to a familiar name from Cruise's past: *Risky Business* producer David Geffen. The novel is the oral history of a 200-year-old vampire named Louis, a beautiful bummer who spent much of his undead life irritated by his French-born sire Lestat, a tall, blond immortal with a cruel charisma. Rice had written Lestat with Rutger Hauer (*Blade Runner*) in mind, but by 1993, he was nearly fifty—far too old to play the irresistible, androgynous blood-drinker. Instead, she wanted one man for the job: Daniel Day-Lewis. Slender, European, and six-two, he looked the part. The press touted that he and Geffen were in talks, triggering ecstasy in *Interview* fans. But Day-Lewis said no, so vehemently in fact that his agent gave a long interview to *Variety* solely to dispel the rumors.[136]

For the first time since *Top Gun*, Cruise wasn't a film's first choice. He wasn't even its second or third. But Geffen and director Neil Jordan, who had just raised eyebrows with 1992's cross-dressing thriller *The Crying Game*, ultimately rejected Rice's other two suggestions, Jeremy Irons and John Malkovich, as being too niche for their expensive dramedy. Cruise had the box office clout, and as Geffen already knew, both he and Lestat were magnetic, controlling, and seemingly indestructible—the latter of which was about to be tested.

"No Tom Cruise!"

When buzz about Cruise's involvement in *Interview* hit the trades, *LA Times* gossip maven Liz Smith assumed he would be playing the kinder bloodsucker Louis, writing that the casting "makes sense as Cruise has yet to play an out-and-out villain [...]. He might gnaw a few lovely necks, yet retain his essential screen quality—that of a basically nice, sensationally good-looking hero."[137] Four days later, however, she recanted. "From deep inside, however, we are told that Tom will *only* do the movie if he plays the lead character, the vampire Lestat. So, recent speculation here was incorrect. It seems Tom Cruise *does* have a yen to play a villainous type, after all."[138] Added an unknown source in *Variety*, "It's the good prince flexing his muscles as an actor [...] it's the first time in his career he's going to take on a dark actor's role."[139]

Note the irony: Cruise, who had risen in the ranks as a psychopath, greaser, and arsonist, was now seen as a one-note hero. His all-American, big box office image made people whitewash even his very recent past as the shallow antagonist of *The Color of Money*, the money-grubbing heartbreaker of *Cocktail* (1988), and even the dastardly salesman in *Rain Man*, who spends the first hour and a half abusing his kidnapped, mentally handicapped brother. (The idea that Cruise was "finally" playing a villain would stalk him through 2004's *Collateral*.) Just three years later, his bleak Oscar-nominated performance in *Born on the Fourth of July* was ancient history to an industry that remembers only your most recent flops and hits—and for Cruise in 1993, those were his indulgent Irish period piece *Far and Away* (1992), and his clumsy but wildly popular popcorn thriller *The Firm*, which *LA Weekly* called "a regression not just for Cruise the actor or Cruise the star, but Cruise the adult."[140]

Once again, Cruise had to prove he belonged alongside the likes of Daniel Day-Lewis. What better way than poaching the part that his competitor had abandoned? "It's not that I feel I've gotta break out to find a mass murderer to

Bloodthirsty: Tom Cruise
in Neil Jordan's *Interview
with the Vampire* (1994).

65

play at this stage," insisted Cruise to *GQ*, adding that he also was open to playing gay parts if the character had payoff.[141] But he was smart enough to know that with Lestat, he could play both: a sexually ambiguous killer.

Just as he did for *Born*, Cruise cut millions from his rate to sweeten the deal. Vampire fans were in shock. Cruise wasn't tall, blond, European, and androgynous—he was a short, dark-haired, all-American jock. "This will probably provide as much controversy as whether Michael Keaton should have played Batman," wrote *Variety* of his casting.[142] Oh, no—this was going to get much worse. As Neil Jordan sighed, "We cast Tom, and all hell broke loose."[143]

Rice went on a rampage. "I was particularly stunned by the casting of Cruise, who is no more my Vampire Lestat than Edward G. Robinson is Rhett Butler," she vented to the *LA Times*. "Cruise should do himself and everyone else a service and withdraw."[144] For nearly two decades, she'd sweated to bring her favorite character to the screen—and now she was on a one-woman crusade to destroy the film if the producers didn't recast Lestat. "The movie could be one of the biggest disasters of all time," she said in a veiled threat, as she presided over rallies of readers chanting, "No Tom Cruise!" and collected petitions promising to boycott the movie.[145] Addressing a thousand-plus audience outside of a book signing on Halloween, Rice hollered, "I wanted to call David Geffen and say, 'How the hell could you do this?'"[146]

"You don't usually start a movie with someone not wanting you to do it," said Cruise, who called Rice's attacks "hurtful" before retreating into his intensive preparation.[147] "Maybe to other people, it looks as if I haven't challenged myself as an actor, but every step of the way, I've pushed myself as hard as I could."[148] Instead of getting drawn into the public brawl, he let the filmmakers fight. "She's not about anything but self-importance. She is hurting people. It's just nasty and gratuitous and uncalled for,"[149] said Geffen, sniping, "If you let fans make the movies, as opposed to the people who make them, then you wouldn't have ended up with *The Godfather* [1972] because back then Al Pacino was just this thin little guy."[150] Added Jordan, "It's pure snobbery when people think European actors have more class or authenticity than their American counterparts."[151]

"Do any of you people actually read?" seethed Rice in a public letter to *People* magazine. "When you're talking Lestat, you're talking Captain Ahab, Custer, Peter the Great. It's that kind of a class act."[152] "I think the real leap of faith is putting Lestat in the company of Peter the Great and Captain Ahab," countered Cruise's press rep Pat Kingsley. Caught in the middle, *People* stayed agnostic, writing, "*People* Magazine extends Anne Rice its best wishes, and has no desire to find out what she's like when she's *really* upset."[153]

"None of this is new," sighed Cruise's agent, Paula Wagner. "People had much the same reaction when Tom was cast as Ron Kovic in *Born on the Fourth of July*."[154] Geffen loudly predicted that *Interview* would score Cruise another Oscar nod, as well as a Best Picture nomination. First, however, they had to shoot the actual movie while surrounded by the most insane tabloid coverage any of them had ever seen. And much of the filming would be done in New Orleans—Rice's hometown.

Tom Cruise was nervous. "I was scared to death when my wife [Nicole Kidman] and I were talking about going down to New Orleans," he admitted. "I didn't know what kind of people would be there waiting for us."[155] Cruise demanded that a covered tunnel be built to connect his trailer to the closed set, starting rumors that he'd received death threats. After River Phoenix, cast as the titular Interviewer, died just days before his first scenes, the press deemed the movie jinxed. They nicknamed it *Cruise's Coffin* and *Geffen's Grave*.

"Fear drove me into it," said Cruise. As ever, he'd done his homework. "I've never worked so hard on a character," he insisted, a curious statement so soon after *Born*.[156] First he began with the physical: he lost eighteen pounds to get Lestat's cadaverous frame, shoved itchy contacts in his eyes, streaked his hair blond, and dyed gold flecks into his eyebrows. He traveled to Versailles to get a feel for the period furniture and fashions of Lestat's youth, practiced Lestat's sinuous and confident movements, and read out loud from classic novels until the romantic diction felt natural. (In an interview with *Us* magazine, Cruise had just credited Scientology with helping him cope with his dyslexia.)

Cruise's second improbable claim was that he hadn't tinkered with the script. He'd proudly added his input to nearly every film since *Losin' It*—why now pretend to be a mere a hired gun, especially when his costar Brad Pitt, a handsome Oklahoman who had just spun a memorable role in 1991's *Thelma and Louise* into a major career, was sounding off to *Rolling Stone* that Cruise was "demanding complete control"?[157] Answer: to blunt Rice's claims that the shy, sex scene–averse actor had toned down the script's homosexual subtext. "Ridiculous!" Kingsley told his accusers. "It's the same script Daniel Day-Lewis would have done."[158] Added Geffen, "He has not had any input into this script whatsoever […]. Any homophobia being alleged against Tom is an outrage and a bald-faced lie."[159]

As if to prove the point, seven months before the film's release Cruise took the stage at Harvard's Hasty Pudding awards wearing a satin bra and pink pumps, and assured anyone who would listen that he was no bigot. "This is the way I feel about the homoerotic issue: I don't care either way," he said. "I don't care if people

Opposite: Anne Rice's novel, on which the screenplay was based, was first published in May 1976.

Anne Rice wasn't alone in her anger. *Interview with the Vampire*'s Cruise crisis was a public frenzy. Before Cruise even put on his Lestat costume, ordinary fans were outraged by his casting. Below is a sampling of their letters to the editor, published in the *Los Angeles Times* on August 29 and September 5, 1993.

"Fans of *Interview with the Vampire*, be they Cruise fans or not, must surely be aghast at his casting as Lestat. The milk-and-cookies star has neither the physical presence nor the range as an actor to effectively play the role. Think of Dana Carvey as Dirty Harry, and you can see how implausible is the casting of Cruise as Lestat. Cruise flashing those fangs for the first time will likely engender unwarranted laughter from the audience, just as Carvey as Dirty Harry would saying 'Make my day.'"
—Jeff Softley, Los Angeles

"Cruise as Lestat? Why not Bugs Bunny or Sylvester the Cat, and make it a real cartoon. Tom Cruise—never!"
—Gary Manning, Hollywood

"I concur, as would anyone with any taste and insight, that the Vampire Lestat must be played by someone with maturity, character, pathos, and vulnerability, not a pasty-faced weakling. What a shame. A marvelous story and movie are being ruined."
—Michael H. Sukoff, Santa Ana

"I felt like I'd been slapped when I heard Cruise would play Lestat. There is a person who walks this Earth who was born to play this part, and that person is none other than Christopher Walken."
—Rebecca Ehrich, San Diego

"Cruise as the Vampire Lestat is inspired. To compliment this brilliance, Jordan and Geffen should consider cameos by Beavis and Butt-head. Heh-heh-heh."
—Michael Roberts, Twentynine Palms

"Sinewy, European, androgynous? How about David Bowie?"
—Tod Shacklett, Etiwanda

"Do these fanatics from Central Casting actually believe vampires exist? Is there really a cast-in-stone role model for a flying bat? Would Gary Oldman's teeth chomping on a neck truly be more *realistic* than Cruise's canines, or even David Letterman's?"
—Robert Tilem, Reseda

Interview With The Vampire
A Novel by Anne Rice

are Martians. I really don't care. Straight. Gay. Bisexual. Catholic. Jewish." In mild exasperation, he sighed, "Look at all the stuff that I've heard about myself. That I'm a misogynist. I'm a homosexual. I'm brainless. How can I be all of these things? So you've just got to go, 'Hey! What the fuck!'"[160]

The shoot was physically and emotionally exhausting. Lestat and Louis are nocturnal creatures, so for nearly four months the crew filmed during the night. "We almost ended up living like vampires," said Jordan, who watched Cruise increasingly identify with Lestat. "In a strange way, the world of a vampire is not that different from the world of a massive Hollywood star. You're kept from the harsh daylight; you live in a strange kind of seclusion. Every time you emerge, a tremendous ripple runs through people," described Jordan, adding, "To me, it was kind of an interesting metaphor: star, vampire, vampire, star. As well as eternal youth. They're condemned to be eternally youthful in a way."[161]

That line between fantasy and reality was blurring in the relationship between the in-control Cruise and the passive Pitt, whose characters complimented their own personas. "When he comes on the set, the set works differently. It changes the rotation of the planets a bit," said Pitt.[162] "I started really resenting him. In retrospect, I realize that it was completely because of who our characters are."[163] At one point, Pitt was so desperate to quit that he asked Geffen what it would cost him. $40 million, said Geffen. Pitt stayed.

The Real Lestat

Interview with the Vampire is told from Louis' point of view. Yet over Anne Rice's entire series, readers realize that Louis, a guilt-stricken vampire who eats rats and poodles, is more a mopey brat than a trustworthy narrator. Unlike Jordan—and especially unlike Pitt, who'd thrown his copy of *Interview* in the trash half-read—Cruise had devoured all four of Rice's Lestat books, and his research subverted Louis' descriptions of Lestat. "There are hints about who Lestat is," Cruise said about *Interview*, "but you hear it all from Louis' viewpoint."[164] To Louis—and in many ways, in the movie— Lestat is a remorseless, manipulative killer. But to Cruise, Lestat was the hero.

Cruise's performance is informed by a history found only in the other books. In *Interview*, Lestat alludes to his troubled past, but refuses to go into detail. "Lestat's a very difficult role because he is an incredibly internalized character," said Cruise.[165] It's not about what he does—it's about why he does it. Yet he doesn't bother trying to win Louis over with sappy explanations. What Cruise knew that Pitt didn't was that Louis was Lestat's *third* vampire

transformation. Before he met Louis, he turned both his mother, who left him, and his best friend Nicolas, a depressive who went insane and lit himself on fire. "He's really a terribly lonely character," noted Cruise.[166] "Everything that Lestat does he does out of love and longing—yet he's sadistic."[167] He saw that Lestat's goading Louis to cheer up is his way of precluding another suicidal abandonment. When Lestat rails at Louis for starving himself, he's not angry—he's hurt, and Cruise presses the viewer to draw a distinction that our narrator can't recognize.

Although salacious readers of the books imagine Louis and Lestat as lovers, onscreen Lestat treats Louis as a son and a student. Playing a vampire—especially one that the script itself presents as a jerk—would have permitted Cruise to be wholly vile. But like a father, Cruise saves his character's anger for when Louis puts himself in danger by setting their mansion on fire, allowing a victim to scream for help, and refusing to eat.

"Everyone was saying to me, 'Oh, Lestat's so evil.' And I remember thinking, 'Jesus, are these people looking at the same character that I'm looking at?'" said Cruise, noting the irony that audiences—and Louis—expect Lestat to act human when he is anything but. By definition, vampirism means drinking human blood—to ask anything different of Lestat would be like demanding that a fish breathe air. "Lestat believes what he is doing is correct," insisted Cruise. "And as a vampire, it is correct."[168]

Yet Cruise's efforts to do right by his character hamper the actual film and expose its weaknesses. Lestat is meant to represent callow bloodlust and Louis the tortured soul. But if audiences think Lestat is likable—and thanks to Cruise, they do—then Louis becomes an unappreciative drag. When Pitt mumbles, "Forgive me if I have a lingering respect for life," a line that should earn empathy, Cruise is so exasperated by his willful stubbornness that Louis seems gratingly naïve.

Cruise's battle to control the audience's sympathies didn't go unnoticed, particularly by Rice. "I'm puzzled by what seems to be a discrepancy between the way Tom played Lestat, and the way my hero, Producer David Geffen, and others have described Lestat as a character. Did Tom on his own make this role a little bigger, brighter and more complex than anyone else realized it could be?" she questioned. "Since he isn't all that nasty, why does Louis hate Lestat? How can he?"[169]

"He really does love Louis," insisted Cruise, and in his character's visible, building frustration with Pitt lies the story's true pain.[170] Lestat is pouring his love into a depressive who will never love him back. His desperation to make Louis embrace his true self—and him in return—leads to the film's greatest scene: Lestat's torture of a prostitute.

Lestat (Tom Cruise) saves Louis (Brad Pitt) from suicide and brings him eternal despair.

Following pages: Tom Cruise and Brad Pitt on the set. Artistic and temperamental differences between the two nearly drove Pitt to walk out of the movie.

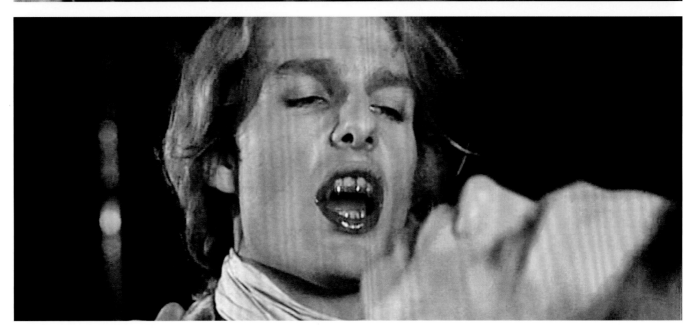

Sex and Power

The girl's drawn-out death starts as playful cruelty, but Cruise's anger mounts at Louis' refusal to act. And if there's one thing a Cruise character doesn't do, it's refuse to act. But Louis won't kill her for food and he won't kill her for mercy. He won't even give Lestat the satisfaction of reacting. "End her suffering! End yours!" Lestat yells. Louis won't, so when Lestat finally drains her life, he's both a killer and a hero.

The masterful four-minute scene, which took a week to shoot, is shockingly sensual and horrifically violent. For Cruise, the most difficult thing to project seems to be eroticism. The oddity of Cruise's career is that his good looks don't translate into sex appeal. His back-lit *Top Gun* seduction of Kelly McGillis is memorable only for the awkward way he licks her face—it's a relief when he puts his clothes back on. Despite being voted *People*'s Sexiest Man Alive in 1990, Cruise's appeal is best summed up by Jeffrey Katzenberg asking his Disney animators to make him the face of Aladdin: he's appealing and safe.

"Everything is about sex except sex," declared Oscar Wilde. "Sex is about power." Power has never been Cruise's problem, and in channeling it, he makes Lestat—a cold-blooded creature weary of sex—seem hot-blooded and passionate. Cruise doesn't kiss a single person in *Interview*, but it's his most sexual performance. Watch the way he casually, comfortably dominates the doomed prostitute: climbing on her body, stroking her face, maintaining his unnerving eye contact.

"I think vampires are very sexy creatures. And I think the idea of being lower on the food chain than someone else is a very terrifying idea,"[171] admitted Cruise, and his linking of eroticism and death fuels his Lestat. Each time he kills, Cruise's Lestat kills uniquely, be it by plunging his teeth into the neck, sucking lightly through the wrist, or nuzzling under the breast. "Each kill has to tell the story of that relationship," he said. "The hard part is learning to bite someone in a different way each time."[172]

The horror of the prostitute torture scene is its combination of physical, psychological, and emotional violence. Lestat doesn't just kill the girl, he destroys her—and Cruise's dexterity adds a chill. Squeezing blood from her arm into a cocktail glass, he doesn't spill a drop. His skillful care hints that he's killed women like that for decades while subliminally underscoring Lestat's respect for his victim's sacrifice. Contrast that to Louis, who angrily dashes the cup to the floor and wastes the girl's final offering.

However, the most shocking contrast comes from Cruise's added dash of black comedy. He teases the girl that she'd look lovely on a bed of satin—read: a coffin—a line that another actor might have read as a threat. Instead, Cruise is playful. "Even in Lestat's darkest moment of pain,

Opposite: In one's blood:
Lestat helps himself to a lady
of the night (Indra Ove).

The vampire and his
protégée (played by a young
Kirsten Dunst).

he is still very witty," insisted Cruise.[173] When
he shoves her in the coffin, he leaps on the lid
and grins. He's testing every emotion—violence,
callowness, delight—to see what will make Louis
respond, and when those don't, Cruise spins
the lid off the coffin with a flourish, then jokes
cheerfully to his victim that she must already be
dead. "Tom's combination of cruelty and humor
was extraordinary here," said Jordan. "It's played
like comedy, I suppose, in the end—appealing to a
vampire to save a life."[174]

Claudia's Revenge

Cruise's deft physicality adds to our enjoyment—
and fear—of Lestat. He's a killer who's delighted
by his kills. When he slays a rat, he pets its head
before biting its neck, then gives the corpse a good
shake as though it were a stubborn jar of jam.
Discovering a desperately hungry Louis about to
devour a human, and an orphaned child at that,
Cruise's reaction isn't sarcastic or self-inflatedly
justified—he's elated, so happy that he grabs the
girl's dead mother and dances.

Lestat turns the little girl into a vampire,
which gives Cruise a second chance to show
Lestat's unappreciated softness. Cruise, who had
just become a father himself to his and Nicole
Kidman's adopted daughter Isabella, dotes on
the girl even more than he allows with Louis.
When Claudia (played by then-eleven-year-old

Kirsten Dunst) kills her piano teacher, the script
calls for Lestat to scold her. But Cruise does so
indulgently, beaming with pride. Meanwhile,
Claudia is growing up and learning that she's
doomed to be a child forever. While both Louis
and Lestat are equally to blame—Louis for biting
her, Lestat for saving her "life"—in keeping with
Interview's myopic view, she seeks vengeance
only on Lestat.

Claudia's murder of Lestat is a simple revenge
arc: he wronged her, so she makes him pay. But
Cruise makes it more complex: by earning our
empathy, he's made her the betrayer. Though
Claudia claims that she must kill Lestat for her and
Louis' freedom, Cruise makes her look like a liar.
His wounded, unappreciated Lestat is already
willing to let them go. Still, he hopes they'll come
around. When Claudia starts her assassination
ploy by bringing him a human gift, Cruise's eyes
show Lestat's surprise that someone has finally
done something nice for him for the first time
in the film. Though he can't resist needling her
that he hopes the gift is "a beautiful woman
with endowments you'll never possess," his face
immediately flushes with guilt.

Cruise's eagerness in the scene is
heartbreaking. In that moment, we realize that
while Lestat is capable of love, he's never been
loved back. "We forgive each other then?" he asks
hesitantly. Yet the twin boys she's brought are
poisoned and fatal, even to a vampire.

(Rice offered to make them a straight couple, but neither Jordan nor Cruise was afraid of the implications of pedophilia.) "You let me drink dead blood," Cruise rasps as he calls for help. As ever, Louis stands uselessly in the corner, his inaction a double betrayal.

A Veteran of Agony

With Cruise "killed" off, *Interview with the Vampire* suffers. It's duller without his energy, though interestingly it's only in Pitt's scenes with Antonio Banderas's vampire Armand that the homosexual subtext of the film shifts to the forefront. Yet Louis and Lestat are doomed to meet again, and if Cruise had left any doubt that he—not Pitt—was the heart of the film, he hammers it home in their final scene.

In it, Louis—now in the 1990s—tracks Lestat to an abandoned mansion where the weakened vampire is stuck in a wheeled chair and reduced to eating rats. The scene is meant to celebrate Louis' power over his wicked creator, but Cruise's Lestat is tremulously forgiving. When he skitters away in sad fear, and panics at a noisy helicopter, he's the battle-scarred Ron Kovic of the undead, a veteran of centuries of agony. Who else (save for Daniel Day-Lewis perhaps) could project such a powerful, physical presence while chair-bound? Lestat begs Louis for help, and Pitt's blankness makes the hero look like the true sociopath. What's meant to be Louis' triumph is actually Lestat's—with Cruise in command of the scene, there's no question that he's the real victim.

Despite his character being called a monster, a villain, a murderer, and just plain "nasty," as David Geffen described him, Cruise gave *Interview with the Vampire* a new—if possibly counterproductive—depth.[175] Though it's Pitt's narration and Pitt's story, it's Cruise's face on the poster, despite his absence from the film's entire third act. In the book, agonized Louis might be the more sympathetic. But on film, it Lestat who audiences want to see again. It makes sense that the film ends with Cruise's Lestat at the wheel of a convertible—and the franchise.

Rice's Change of Heart

Interview with the Vampire was a sensation, the biggest opening box office weekend of 1994. It immediately had its champions and detractors, including Oprah Winfrey, who walked out after ten minutes saying, "I don't want to be a contributor to the force of darkness."[176] Still, there was only one person whose opinion mattered: Anne Rice. And she was thrilled.

In a six-page, personally paid-for advertisement in *Variety*, she gushed about Cruise's performance. "From the moment he appeared, Tom was Lestat for me. He has the immense physical and moral presence; he was defiant and yet never without conscience; he was beautiful beyond description, yet compelled to do cruel things. The sheer beauty of Tom was dazzling, but the polish of his acting, his flawless plunge into the Lestat person, his ability to speak rather boldly poetic lines, and speak them with seeming ease and conviction were exhilarating and uplifting. The guy is great. I'm no good at modesty. I like to believe Tom's Lestat will be remembered the way Olivier's *Hamlet* is remembered."[177]

A frail, chair-bound Lestat recalls Ron Kovic.

5

Jerry Maguire

Jerry Maguire (1996)
Cameron Crowe

"Breakdown? Break*through*."
—Jerry Maguire

"Where is all this heading for you?" Cameron Crowe asked Tom Cruise before they teamed up to shoot *Jerry Maguire*. "I'm looking for overall growth," replied Cruise. "But I enjoy working with writers and their scripts."[178]

Their frank talk took place in 1986, prior to the premiere of *Top Gun* and three years before journalist Cameron Crowe was to direct his first film, *Say Anything...* (1989). The *Interview* magazine Q&A was for Cruise's first-ever cover story—he'd come to Crowe's attention while visiting his friend Sean Penn on the set of *Fast Times at Ridgemont High* (1982), Crowe's first screenwriting credit. ("I remember the baby-faced Cruise, unknown but still charged with obvious charisma," recalled Crowe ten years later.[179]) Neither man knew then that they'd meet again in exactly one decade to shoot *Jerry Maguire*, a modest $50 million romantic dramedy about a sports agent stricken with a conscience that vaulted into the public consciousness with five Oscar nominations and three poppy catchphrases: "You complete me," "You had me at 'hello,'" and "Show me the money!"

Even then, their collaboration felt fated. In that first feature, Crowe called *Risky Business* "a perfect showcase for Cruise's style—equal parts comic vulnerability and dramatic strength," and when he asked Cruise what he thought the film was about, Cruise gave him a mini-version of Jerry Maguire's mission statement. "Today's capitalistic society," answered the then-twenty-four-year-old Cruise. "Do you want to help people, or do you just want to make money?"[180]

Ten years later *Jerry Maguire* would wrestle with the same question. In fact, Maguire could be the smooth-talking Joel Goodsen all grown-up. What if after Joel Goodsen studied business at Yale, he scored a fast-paced job as a sports agent, landed another hot girlfriend, and continued living the American dream—until he began to wonder if he'd taken the wrong path? Despite their parallels, when Crowe first began mapping out *Jerry Maguire*'s script, he didn't intend it for Tom Cruise—he was writing it for Tom Hanks. But the story took over three years to complete. Crowe immersed himself in the world of NFL deals and sneaker endorsements. By the end of his process, Hanks had not only aged out of the role, he'd won two Best Actor Oscars in quick succession, plus the clout to direct his next picture, *That Thing You Do!* (1996), himself. Which is what he did.

Crowe called Cruise. It wasn't wholly out of the blue—years before, Cruise had recognized Crowe's name in the credits of *Say Anything...* and phoned him with his congratulations. "I thought, 'Cameron Crowe! Is that the same Cameron Crowe who was a journalist?'" he recalled. "'This guy's really talented.'"[181] When he read the *Jerry Maguire* script, Cruise cried. He called Crowe again, and the two talked for an hour about the character. For Cruise, *Maguire* was reminiscent of his earlier work in *Risky Business* and *Rain Man*—the kind of role he was eager to get back to after his succession of well-received popcorn flicks like *Interview with the Vampire* and *Mission: Impossible*.

"He seemed most impressed that I had taken three and a half years to write the script," observed Crowe. Yet neither man was ready to commit. In the public's eye, Cruise was the superhumanly cool Ethan Hunt of *Mission: Impossible*, which had just made $467.7 million at the global box office. It had been several years since he'd played a regular guy in a tie, and that's if you consider mob boss–fighting Mitch McDeere in 1993's *The Firm* "regular." As for Crowe, he wasn't convinced Cruise would say yes. "Agents of other actors called regularly, saying all kinds of things to promote their clients from, 'Be realistic, you'll never get Cruise,' to, 'Cruise will never play a loser.'"[182]

"Do you really think my image affects people that much? I disagree!" squabbled Cruise to the press. "It's the same thing people were saying about me and Dustin in *Rain Man*: Who would buy us as losers? Do you think I choose characters based on my own image? Image is something I don't understand! I don't get it. It would *never* be why I would make a picture."[183] Instead, he insisted to Crowe that what he really wanted to make was something that wasn't a "Tom Cruise" movie. *Jerry Maguire* was the best of both worlds: a movie about a Tom Cruise type who immediately loses everything and is forced to rebuild.

Tom Cruise as Jerry Maguire, a tormented alpha male sports agent.

The hero and his girlfriend, Dorothy Boyd, played by Renée Zellweger).

Opposite: Director Cameron Crowe (facing the monitor) with Penélope Cruz and Tom Cruise on the set of *Vanilla Sky* (2001), a US remake of Alejandro Amenábar's *Open Your Eyes* (1997).

Cruise sat down with Crowe and producer James L. Brooks for an informal audition. "Who knows if I'm the right guy for this part?" he admitted. "How about if I just read it for you?" Struck by the swagger, depth, and vulnerability of his reading, Crowe was convinced. "Now all I want in the world is for Tom Cruise to be Jerry Maguire," he wrote in his journal.[184]

Still, another two months of talks ticked by as Cruise studied videotapes of sports agents while flying back and forth from Europe, where wife Nicole Kidman was gearing up to shoot *Portrait of a Lady* (1996). In total, Cruise spent eight months prepping the film. "He loves to work and he loves to produce work—he even loves saying the word 'work,'" Crowe joked.[185]

Casting and Character Building

Crowe's main inspiration for *Jerry Maguire* was Billy Wilder's *The Apartment* (1960). "I wanted to write a movie with a real story, the kind that shows up on TV late at night, usually in black and white," he insisted.[186] So he wrote his own dramedy about a working man questioning the value of his work. To make sure audiences caught the connection, Crowe nodded to *The Apartment* with his opening line: just as Jack Lemmon tallied that New York holds 8,042,783 people, Tom Cruise tells us that the world holds six billion people. To fill out the rest of his character, Crowe pulled from Tony Curtis in the *Sweet Smell of Success* (1957) and sports agent Leigh Steinberg, famous for representing Troy Aikman and Oscar de la Hoya.

With Cruise's salary swallowing up $20 million of *Jerry Maguire*'s $50 million budget, Crowe couldn't afford another big name. He chose Sundance starlet Renée Zellweger, a nineties riff on Shirley MacLaine who was then so unknown that Brooks joked to the press, "I'm trying to learn how to spell her last name."[187] Added Crowe, "She caught Tom's attention in an interesting way and when they were together, they looked like an odd couple that might ultimately be a great couple. Renée was always electric when she was in the room with Tom, and she kind of flipped a switch inside him that made him seem more real."[188]

Crowe's ultimate casting goal: convince Billy Wilder himself to cameo as Jerry Maguire's mentor, Dicky Fox. Then eighty-nine years old, Wilder was a near-impossible sell. Yet when Crowe jumped in the car to try to convince the great director to join their film, Cruise insisted on coming along. No luck. After looking askance at Cruise's casual jeans and shirt—in Wilder's day, stars dressed up—Wilder firmly refused. Cruise was respectful but stunned. Mused Crowe, "Perhaps it had been years since he had heard the word 'no' so often and so powerfully in such a short period of time."[189]

Cruise and Crowe's Second Go

Flush with *Jerry Maguire*'s success, Cameron Crowe and Tom Cruise wanted to work together again. The resulting film, *Vanilla Sky*, is a curio that both distills and deconstructs Cruise's screen image. A wealthy publishing scion, Cruise's David Aames is an exaggeration of success: he owns a Manhattan mansion, a $35 million mint condition Ferrari, and the heart of Cameron Diaz. Callow and callous (his office nickname is "Citizen Dildo"), Aames is who his money-grubbing jerks in *Cocktail* and *Rain Man* would have become if they'd won the lotto, a vain party boy who spends his mornings meticulously tweezing his grey hairs and his nights shooting tequila and dancing to trance music. Yet having established that Aames has it all, Crowe eagerly strips his securities away—starting with Cruise's handsome face when Aames is disfigured in a car accident. Like a nightmarish Boschian magnification of *Jerry Maguire*, Aames endures both higher highs and lower lows until the film's head-scratching finale, which posits that true love and true happiness may be nothing more than a mass delusion. Wrote the *Village Voice*, "The new Tom Cruise project, *Vanilla Sky*, may be the most vividly discomfiting star vehicle since *Yentl* [1983]. The faith that it displays in the transcendence of essential Tomness is astonishing. Those eyes, those teeth: With a fervor and passion we haven't quite seen before, Cameron Crowe's movie treats Cruise like a visiting archangel on hormonal overload. Though a by-the-letter remake of Alejandro Amenábar's 1997 Dickian psychodrama *Open Your Eyes*, *Vanilla Sky* is the weirder film, if only because of its contexts: 2001 America, Hollywood, and, most vitally, Tom's brainpan, where human life as we know it is empowered toward glory by the sheer effulgence of the man's generously availed grin. I don't think I've ever seen a movie so hauntingly frank about being a manifestation of its star's cosmic narcissism."[e]

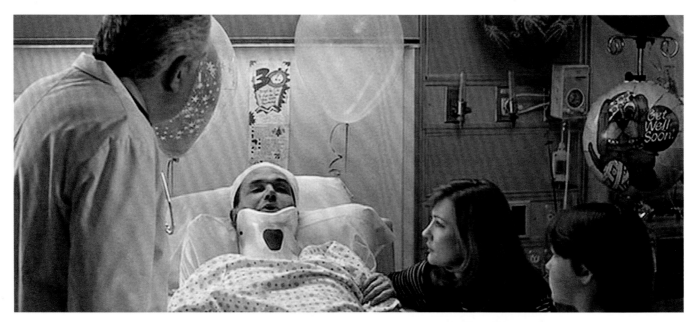

Opposite: Maguire searches
his empty soul when
confronted by the angry son
of an injured athlete.

Cameron Crowe and Tom
Cruise on the set of the film.

Off the set, Cruise was applying his own powers of observation to flesh out his character. Like Maguire, he was used to being around the rich and famous, but he'd almost always been *the* most rich and *the* most famous—not the behind-the-scenes worker who jokes that he always gets cut out of the photo. "You see guys walking down the street in a suit with a cellular phone—I just look at them and think, 'Does he have a family and kids?'" wondered Cruise. "I liked the idea of capturing that—the inner life of a salesman, the businessman. His daily dilemma of moral choices."[190]

Crowe, a former hotshot *Rolling Stone* reporter who would eventually spin his own autobiography into the Oscar-winning *Almost Famous* (2000), paid the actor a personal compliment: "Cruise tirelessly collects the details and behavior on his character, observing and interviewing like a journalist."[191] Both he and Cruise were interested in using *Jerry Maguire* to explore their questions about civilian, white-collar culture—anthropology as worthy of examination as the rock stars Crowe had traveled with on the road. "Guys that put on the tie every day. Where does their poetry come from? How does their soul ever get noticed?" asked Crowe. "They'll say something like, 'I pursue *it* all day long.' But what is *it*? Where is *it*? What is *it*?—Tom Cruise would really key in on that in his performance."[192]

Crowe and Cruise decided to shoot the movie mostly chronologically. The very first scene filmed was Jerry's opening credits revelation that he might be a terrible person, which he learns after the son of an injured client gives him the middle finger. ("That kid couldn't wait to say, 'Fuck you,'" joked Cruise.[193]) Both used music to key into the emotional tenor of a scene. Crowe, a stickler for shaping the perfect sound track, would play music during takes to set the mood—songs that would often wind up in the final film. Meanwhile, before shooting emotionally intense scenes, Cruise would sit alone with a Walkman and dive deep into places "that clearly wrenched him to visit," observed the director, who gave him the space he needed to find Maguire's motivations. "Once he is there, he asks only for quiet. Then he can stay there for as long as it takes, with the world's most sophisticated cameras whirring one inch from his face," wrote Crowe in his filming diary. "Often, I would say to him, 'Do you have another take in you?' 'I have a hundred more in me,' he would say. 'I'll go forever.'"[194]

Jerry Maguire is the ultimate Tom Cruise character: a hotshot, smooth-talking capitalist. But the actual performance is also one of the most unusual of his career. In the film's first minutes, this is classic Cruise—a slick charmer who moves with confidence. But before Crowe's name even appears onscreen in the opening title sequence, Maguire has realized that his job has no value, written a furious manifesto attesting to the fact, immediately regretted said manifesto, and then tiptoed nervously back into the office expecting to be shunned. Instead, his coworkers hail him with a cliché slow clap. He can't hear them secretly snickering, and he smiles and spins triumphantly in the center of the lobby. The scene feels like the end of an eighties movie—say, *Rain Man*, where Cruise's car salesman Charlie Babbitt learns that there's more to life than cash. Yet, in the midst of Maguire's giddy relief, Cruise takes a quick, deep inhale, cluing us in that even he didn't believe redemption would be this easy—and we shouldn't either.

What's striking about *Jerry Maguire* is that it takes the same journey that defined Cruise's early roles—a careerist shark learns humility, falls in love, and discovers his true priorities—and reshuffles it to make the audience realize the whole idea of a life-changing epiphany is bunk. The great irony of Jerry Maguire's status as the signature Tom Cruise role is that it subverts all of his roles that came before. Maguire spends the entire film striving to reclaim the status he willfully discarded in the film's first minutes. It's like a sequel to *Rain Man* in which Babbitt wakes up one morning relieved that he didn't let his autistic brother move in and wreck his bachelor lifestyle.

"Jerry goes through a big transition, but I felt very strongly that you had to see that this guy could be a killer. When he got on those phones at work—you gotta see that he's good at it, because you gotta see what he loses," stressed Cruise.[195] "He spends the rest of the movie denying what he wrote, trying to forget about it, saying, 'That's not really who I am.'"[196] When Maguire moans that he "ate some bad pizza, went to bed, and grew a conscience," Cruise sneers the last word.

On set, Cruise was his usual high-energy demon. Before takes, he'd jump rope in the corner, then run in front of the cameras shouting, "Let's go! Let's fire it up! Let's shoot! Let's rock 'n' roll!" On his mirror next to photos from all of his earlier movies—Cruise wanted to ensure his hair and makeup team gave Maguire a totally original look—he taped a piece of paper with the word "Relax" in bold letters, telling Crowe, "If I'm loose, I can go places I've never been before as an actor. Any time you want, just tell me to relax. It'll help." Crowe did, and upon his command, Cruise would get loose and crazy. Said Crowe, "Those takes are not in the movie, but the next ones are." Cruise color-coded his script with page markers and kept it with him continually. "He knows all of his lines and everybody else's, too," added Crowe.[197] When other actors tried to improvise, it was Cruise—not Crowe—who steered them back in line, saying, "Let's do the scene as written, because, hey, the script is great."[198]

Yet Cruise was also game to get loose when Crowe would change dialogue on the spur of the moment, like in Maguire's desperate phone call montage where he pleads for his clients to stick with him. Crowe would yell a new line—like, say, Maguire denying racial allegations by calling himself "*Mr.* Black People"—and Cruise would immediately spit it back out with conviction. "Writing on the fly. It's like playing jazz," laughed Cruise.[199] In turn, he helped Crowe come up with lines for five-year-old Jonathan Lipnicki, whose blurting out of random facts ("The human head weighs eight pounds") was inspired by his own two young children.

A Sort of Romantic Dramedy

Jerry Maguire is pegged as a romantic comedy, though it's really more of a comedy disguised as a drama with a dash of romance. Regardless, it was a fully new genre for Cruise, who had done dramas with some wry humor (*Risky Business*, *Far and Away*) and action films with some romance (*Top Gun*, *Days of Thunder*) but never a film that combined the two—and definitely never one that gave either comedy or romance center stage. The key to Cruise's performance is that his character doesn't know he's in a comedy—Jerry Maguire is suffering in his own soul-searching drama. To the audience, Jerry's collapse is funny. To him, it's anguish. Cruise plays the role straight: Jerry can't laugh at himself, but the joke is on him, so much so that when Jerry deliberately tries to tell a joke—like telling wide receiver Rod Tidwell (Cuba Gooding Jr.) to be careful on the field since he's his entire client roster—his humor falls flat.

Although *Jerry Maguire* is best known for launching "Show me the money!" into the public consciousness, to Cruise the dialogue was secondary. "You can't just learn the lines and show up," he insisted. "The easiest thing about being an actor is memorizing lines! The stuff you don't see is the exploration of character."[200] Crowe had filled the script with sharp zingers, but Cruise refused to rely on the lines themselves to make audiences laugh. *Risky Business* had been a comedy without jokes. *Jerry Maguire*, arguably only Cruise's second funny film, wouldn't rely on them either.

Jerry Maguire is a deceptively physical role. The laughs come at small things Cruise does: falling into the bushes, hugging people too fast, shaking his love rival's hand two dozen times, mock sword-fighting his enemies with a fireplace poker, and walking into Dorothy's hanging lamp (which, in order for the five-foot-seven actor to pull off, had to be hung so low it doesn't even make sense). It's almost unnerving to watch Cruise stumble—so much so that on the day Maguire is publicly thrown out of his office and Cruise falls flat on his face, the extras gasped and then started their

After he's fired by Bob Sugar (Jay Mohr) at lunch, Maguire goes from confidence to desperation as he begs his clients to stick with him.

Following pages:
Loneliness and uncertainty for Tom Cruise's character.

own slow clap. "They were not sure they should, but they hailed him for failing," said Crowe with a smile. "As Tom Cruise took a Chaplin-esque bow, I could feel the whole movie sail into uncharted waters. I was watching an actor take his super-icon persona and turn it inside out. I was on a high for days after that fall."[201]

But the implication of Cruise's clumsiness isn't that Maguire is a klutz—it's that Maguire is as unsteady in the world as a newborn deer, and so disoriented that he doesn't notice his surroundings. Crowe shot much of the film in the middle of the night—the sword-fighting scene was filmed at 5 am—and, fittingly, the exhaustion is visible in Cruise's face. What doesn't work in Cruise's performance is the loose-limbed, five-second quivering freak-out in his office when Maguire insists that he's *not* going to freak out—it's a gonzo gesture that would work for Nicolas Cage, but not for a Cruise character who, even when shattered, would never deliberately let himself look uncool. After all, the first thing he does after falling on his face is stand up and straighten his tie.

"In character comedies like this, it's what's *not* said," Cruise noted. "There's a lot of work to get it to that point, where the humor can come just from a look on a guy's face."[202] Cruise still manages to wring laughs from Crowe's dialogue even without actually saying a joke. The secret is in his delivery—and the best examples come when he merely repeats the same words with a twist. Think of his locker room scene where he pleads with Rod Tidwell to try being a little nicer to his fans. Each iteration is a roller coaster of emotions. "*Help* me help you. Help *me* help you. Help me help *you*," he begs. And when he rhetorically presses Tidwell about his love of football ("It wasn't just about the money, was it?") halfway through, Cruise's voice shifts as Maguire begins to question it himself: "*Was it? Was* it?"

During the scene, Cruise studies Cuba Gooding Jr.'s face with an almost uncomprehending and animalistic intensity, as though he's a dog trying to glean what his master needs him to do for a treat. In essence, he's making visible what makes a good agent: being focused on what his client—or their owners—thinks, wants, and succumbs to. As Cruise plays him, Jerry Maguire is cocky, but he's not self-centered—note how eagerly he promises everyone around him that he'll do whatever they need to make them happy. (Plus, note how often his need-to-please gets him in trouble—especially when it means making promises to his on-again, off-again love interest Dorothy.)

And as an agent, his entire measure of success depends on what he's done for other people—and in turn, his sole measure of self-worth is externalized, a truth we learn early on at his bachelor party during a video roast hosted by his ex-girlfriends. As his former flings gush that

he made their hearts pound, Cruise grins like he believes them. But when they accuse him of being a liar who hates to be alone, his smile turns forced, then cold, then collapses into a frown. A true narcissist would immediately convince himself that they're wrong—or he wouldn't care at all. But other people's opinions are the only reflection of himself Maguire has.

A handsome, deft heartthrob, Tom Cruise was always a natural fit for romantic comedies, which is why it's odd that he hadn't—and arguably still hasn't—made one. Part of the painful joke of *Jerry Maguire* is that the wedding is in the second act—and from there, things between Jerry and Dorothy slide downhill. "I haven't found a romantic comedy that I could do,"[203] explained Cruise the year after *Jerry Maguire* came out, as though he, too, refused to accept that it fit in the genre. (That across a three-decade-plus career he hasn't found even one suggests he isn't looking very hard.) Even when you break apart his dramatic films with a love story subplot, the real romance was between Cruise and his plane, Cruise and his car, or Cruise and his career.

Jerry Maguire is in part a response to Cruise's entire career as an accidental ladies' man. Though a half dozen of his biggest hits have ended with his character winning the girl, the love story has always been so secondary that the "happy" ending is merely optimistic. Who really thinks he'll stay with *Cocktail*'s Elisabeth Shue forever—he's already dumped her while she's pregnant—or that in *Top Gun*, he and Kelly McGillis can check their egos long enough to build something lasting? The shelf life on his relationship with Rebecca De Mornay's prostitute in *Risky Business* can be counted in weeks, if not days, and the idea of his callow race car driver in *Days of Thunder* really fulfilling Nicole Kidman's brilliant neurosurgeon is as believable as then-twenty-two-year-old Kidman playing a brilliant neurosurgeon. Though *Jerry Maguire* ends with Cruise and Zellweger literally walking off into the sunset, we're subconsciously primed to doubt that this, too, will last. He's not even holding her hand. Sure, the film ends with Maguire spinning a sudden emotional epiphany into a grandiose, public rant—but that's also how the film begins. And we've already seen how quickly he reneged on those big promises.

"I was never sure about that speech. I just thought, is it too much? Is it too heart-in-hand?" said Crowe of Maguire's big closing speech. But Cruise insisted they give his original draft a shot. Crowe kept an eye on the crew members to see if the moment was working, and he saw three women by the monitor who "were just destroyed." His lead actor was also affected. When Cruise sighs, "We live in a cynical world," Crowe saw a shift in his face. "It was you connecting to it so personally," he later told Cruise. "It was more than just words. It was a feeling."[204]

His secretary's son (Jonathan Lipnicki) is the first person to crack Maguire's narcissistic shell.

Following pages: Tom Cruise and Cuba Gooding, Jr., who plays Rod Tidwell, his sole remaining client.

Opposite: When Maguire's bachelor party/video roast calls him a callow lothario, the joke is so real he stops laughing.

A happy ending? What if Maguire and Boyd's relationship was doomed from the start?

Problems with Intimacy

Parse Maguire's climatic declaration of love, and Cruise's read on the character makes even more sense. Stiff and awkward, Maguire stands literally across the room from his wife—not daring to actually touch her—as he chokes out the famous line, "You complete me." She completes him? Romantic, to be sure—but it also proves that after spending an entire film dwelling on his shallowness, Maguire knows he's still hollow. He started the movie full of empty swagger and lost the swagger, but stayed empty.

As David Denby of *New York* magazine wrote, Cruise "shows us that there's a terrifying abyss under the confidence—no ideas, no particular personality, nothing." [205] Which raises the question: Why does Dorothy like *him*? Is she just another girl who falls sway to Maguire's charisma? Is she, perhaps, as shallow as him? Even in the scenes between him and her son, the only person Maguire truly seems to love, Cruise subtly hints that he's not ready to accept even a child's guileless adoration. He steamrolls over him without making eye contact when the boy tries to talk about his dead father, and when the boy first moves in to give him a kiss, Maguire ever so slightly recoils. It goes without saying that his kisses with Dorothy couldn't be more deliberately awkward—he stiffly pecks her hand and cheek, and even during their first seduction scene,

quickly moves away from the intimacy of her mouth to move lower down her neck and chest.

"I've never had the problem with intimacy that Jerry does," insisted Cruise. "My emotions are very available. I'm an actor, so I'm dealing with that all the time." [206] Once again, he was hitting the awards circuit in an attempt to convince critics and award voters that his work in *Jerry Maguire* was actually acting and not just an extension of himself. And once again it worked, to a point. The film scored Cruise his second Best Actor Golden Globe win and his second Academy Award nomination. But when Oscar night rolled around, Cruise wasn't there—he was across the Atlantic working on a film he hoped would be even more important to his career.

6

Dr. William Harford

Eyes Wide Shut (1999)
Stanley Kubrick

"Now, where exactly are we going... exactly?"
—Dr. Bill Harford

It started with a fax, though neither Tom Cruise nor Nicole Kidman could agree when it was sent. Did they both receive it separately at the same time? Did Tom alone get it the year before? Either way, the fax was from Stanley Kubrick, and it asked Hollywood's most famous couple if they would star in his next film, script TBD.

Actually, it started with *The Firm*. Stanley Kubrick wanted a real-life husband and wife to star in his dream project: a psychological drama that would delve into jealousy and lust. He had a couple in mind—Alec Baldwin and Kim Basinger—though they would be divorced by the time *Eyes Wide Shut* opened in 1999. But Kubrick asked his friend, the director Sydney Pollack, what he thought of that hotshot lawyer from Pollack's last picture, *The Firm*. Was Tom Cruise eager and adaptable? Pollack said yes, not knowing that by the time Kubrick's opus wrapped, he, too, would be dragged into its epic filming schedule for so long that he'd get bored enough to teach Cruise how to cook homemade pasta from scratch.

Stanley Kubrick hadn't made a film since 1987's *Full Metal Jacket*. Before that, he hadn't made a film since 1980's *The Shining*. Cruise, over a decade into his vow to work only with the great directors, was unquestionably eager to star in the new picture from one of the last living classic auteurs. His wife, Nicole Kidman, was finally transitioning from Aussie starlet to serious actress after the one-two success of *To Die For* (1995) and *Portrait of a Lady*. Individually, they had something to prove. Together, the challenge was doubled—both of their previous pairings, *Days of Thunder* and *Far and Away,* were critically panned. They, and their pride, were ready for whatever mystery Kubrick had planned. And they were willing to do anything. Gushed Cruise, "It's just a damned miracle that he wanted me and Nic to do this."[207]

What they later learned is that Kubrick had wanted to make *Eyes Wide Shut* for thirty years. After *Lolita* (1962), he chose Arthur Schnitzler's 1926 erotic drama *Traumnovelle*, the loose inspiration for the film, as his next project. But his own wife, the painter Christiane Kubrick,

said no. They'd been married for only four years—their marriage couldn't handle it, she feared. Kubrick clung to the idea. "Whenever he brought it up, I'd say, 'I hate that book—put it away,'"[208] said Christiane, but after three happy decades together, she finally consented. Only seven years into their marriage, Cruise and Kidman were confident they were emotionally up for the challenge.

Kubrick had a script. He asked cowriter Frederic Raphael for so many rewrites that Raphael eventually penned an exasperated tell-all called *Eyes Wide Open*, in which he seemed convinced that Kubrick's only goal for the film was to destroy his collaborator before shooting even started. The structure closely follows *Traumnovelle*: after his wife confesses to an unacted-upon fantasy about a stranger, a husband embarks on an oddly neutered sexual odyssey in which he considers—but never consummates—physical relationships with his patient's daughter, a prostitute, a teenager, and a stranger at an orgy. Upon Kubrick's request, Raphael translated the story from turn-of-the-century Vienna to modern-day Manhattan and fleshed out the characters as wealthy WASPs Bill and Alice Harford. But Raphael noticed that Kubrick's revisions stripped the Harfords of their individuality. "I came to realize that he didn't even want the characters to have any particular personality," noted Raphael, "he would as soon have types as individuals with specific histories or sensibilities." Additionally, the director shunned clever dialogue ("It was not something he wanted to film"), character motivations ("Kubrick left motive or 'psychology' to be divined by the spectator"), and even a clear story arc ("Anything too finished left him with an obligation to obedience").[209]

"I was now compiling a color-it-yourself book in which the spaces might have seductive outlines but were not to carry any instructions,"[210] complained Raphael. With the script pared down to its essence, the weight of filling in the characters—not to mention making their story compelling—now rested on Cruise and Kidman.

For fifteen months, the *Eyes Wide Shut* set was a mystery. It still is. Kubrick refused to let anyone—even the studio executives at Warner Bros.—read the script. He wanted the final film

Dr. Bill Harford in Stanley Kubrick's *Eyes Wide Shut* (1999).

95

to speak for itself, so he shunned interviews during the filming process and agreed to do only a few just before the film was released. But Kubrick died before he could speak openly about the film, leaving only his widow to speak for him when she insists he thought it was his masterpiece.

In Camera with the Auteur

Kubrick's obsession with secrecy so infected his cast and crew that no one has ever spoken about it in detail. The day-to-day life on set can only be inferred from facts and hints. The most major fact: *Eyes Wide Shut* was exhausting. Kubrick had asked Cruise and Kidman to commit to six months. When they landed in London in the fall of 1996, the couple fully expected to return to Hollywood by spring. Instead, they stayed on through the summer, fall, and another Christmas. Filming wrapped in January of 1998, but in May they were summoned back for more months of reshoots. Altogether they'd spend 400 days on *Eyes Wide Shut*, the Guinness world record for the longest continual film shoot.

"Stanley had figured out a way to work in England for a fraction of what we pay here," explained Pollack, who joined the cast as the corrosive tycoon Victor Ziegler after the extended shooting forced original actor Harvey Keitel to cry uncle and drop out. "While the rest of us poor bastards are able to get 16 weeks of filming for $70 million with a $20 million star, Stanley could get 45 weeks of shooting for $65 million."[211] Though every six months Cruise spent in London cost him another $20 million film he wasn't making—plus he had the fledgling Cruise/Wagner production company to oversee—he swore to the press he had no qualms about his extended art house sabbatical.

"I remember talking to Stanley and I said, 'Look, I don't care how long it takes, but I have to know: are we going to finish in six months?'" said Cruise. "People were waiting and writers were waiting. I'd say, 'Stanley, I don't care—tell me it's going to be two years.'"[212]

Kubrick is legendary for his perfectionism—to reconstruct Greenwich Village in London, he sent a designer to New York to measure the exact width of the streets and the distance between newspaper vending machines. But his approach to character and performance was the opposite. Instead of knowing what he wanted on the set, he waited for the actors to seize upon it themselves. His process: repeated takes designed to break down the idea of performance altogether. The theory was that once his actors bottomed-out in exhaustion and forgot about the cameras, they could rebuild and discover something that neither he nor they expected. During *The Shining*, he'd put Jack Nicholson and Shelley Duvall through fifty takes to figure out what he wanted, causing

Duvall to have a nervous breakdown. For *Eyes Wide Shut*, given his stars' extreme pliancy and eagerness to please, Kubrick went further, once insisting that Cruise do ninety-five takes of walking through a door.

"In times when we couldn't get it, it was just like, 'Fuck!'" admitted Cruise. "I'd bring it upon myself because I demand a lot of myself."[213] But what he never asked—at least, not openly in the press—was if there was an "it" Kubrick wanted him to get. After all, a director who demands ninety-five takes could be exacting—or conversely, he could be ill-prepared and uncommunicative. Cruise's overpreparation had served him well in the past. Not here. He got an ulcer, and tried to keep the news from Kubrick. At its core, the Cruise/Kubrick combination seems cruel: an overachieving actor desperate to please a never-satisfied auteur. The power balance was firmly shifted to Kubrick, yet to his credit, Cruise has never complained.

Kubrick defenders—Cruise included—insist the legend was fully in command. "He was not indulgent," Cruise insisted to the press.[214] "You know you are not going to leave that shot until it's right."[215] Yet it's hard not to see indulgence when even small roles demanded prolonged commitment, like starlet Vinessa Shaw's one-scene cameo as a prostitute, which was meant to take two weeks and ended up wasting two months. Adding to the peril, Kubrick also refused to screen dailies, a practice Cruise relied on. "Making a movie is like stabbing in the dark," the actor explained. "If I get a sense of the overall picture, then I'm better for the film."[216] Cruise couldn't watch and adjust his performance to find his character's through line—a problem exacerbated by the amount of footage the director filmed. For most of the cast, who appeared only in one or two moments, they had only to match the timbre of their character's big moment. But Cruise alone is in nearly every scene and had to spend the shoot playing a guessing game. Not knowing which of his mind-melting number of takes would wind up in the film, he still had to figure out how to shape a consistent character from scene-to-scene. Given Kubrick's withholding direction and the exponential number of combinations that could be created from his raw footage, it's understandable if the forever-prepared actor found himself adrift.

Adding to the actor's peril was the part's personal and emotional risk. Kubrick decided to find his story through psychoanalyzing his stars, prodding Cruise and Kidman to confess their fears about marriage and commitment to their director in conversations that the three vowed to keep secret. "Tom would hear things that he didn't want to hear," admitted Kidman. "It wasn't like therapy, because you didn't have anyone to say, 'And how do you feel about that?'

Opposite, top: Dr. Harford and his wife, Alice (Nicole Kidman), with their daughter, Helena (Madison Eginton).

Opposite, bottom: Cruise with director Stanley Kubrick.

Following pages: Victor Ziegler (Sydney Pollack) confronts Bill Harford.

Tom Cruise's character entertains serious doubts about his marriage.

Opposite: Alice's sex fantasy scene took six days to shoot. (Cruise was banned from the set.)

It was honest, and brutally honest at times."[217] The line between reality and fiction was deliberately blurred. The couple slept in their characters' bedroom, chose the colors of the curtains, strewed their clothes on the floor, and even left pocket change on the bedside table just as Cruise did at home.

"As an actor, you set up: there's reality, and there's pretend," explained Kidman. "And those lines get crossed, and it happens when you're working with a director that allows that to happen. It's a very exciting thing to happen; it's a very dangerous thing to happen."[218] Added Cruise, "I wanted this to work, but you're playing with dynamite when you act. Emotions kick up."[219] At least the two actors had an auditory cue to distinguish fact from fiction: on camera, Kidman changed her Australian accent to American. But there was also external tension pressing down on their performances, as both actors—especially Cruise—were media savvy enough to recognize that audiences would project Bill and Alice's unhappiness on their own marriage, which was already a source of tabloid fodder. Even during the course of filming, the couple had to sue *Star* magazine (successfully) for writing that they hired sex therapists to teach them how to kiss.

Kubrick's on-set wall of secrecy even divided Cruise and Kidman. To exaggerate the distrust between their fictional husband and wife,

Kubrick would direct each actor separately and forbid them to share notes. In one painful example, for just one minute of final footage where Alice makes love to a handsome naval officer—an imaginary affair that haunts Bill over the course of the film—Kubrick demanded that Kidman shoot six days of naked sex scenes with a male model. Not only did he ask the pair to pose in over fifty erotic positions, he banned Cruise from the set and forbade Kidman to assuage her husband's tension by telling him what happened during the shoot.

Costar Vinessa Shaw would eventually admit Kubrick had exhausted the once-indefatigable actor, confessing that compared to Cruise's "gung ho" first months of shooting, by the end, "He was still into it, but not as energetic."[220] Still, when *LA Times* gossip columnist Liz Smith wrote that the *Eyes Wide Shut* set was miserable, Cruise quickly fired back a letter insisting that his and Kidman's relationship with Kubrick was "impeccable and extraordinary. [...] Both Nic and I love him."[221] Added actor and director Todd Field, on set for six months to play the pivotal role of the piano player Nick Nightingale, "You've never seen two actors more completely subservient and prostrate themselves at the feet of a director."[222] However, Cruise's devotion to Kubrick's massive mystery masterpiece would prove damaging to his screen image.

Between fiction and reality: The Cruise/Kidman relationship, as seen through the director's lens.

Opposite: Stanley Kubrick, Tom Cruise, Nicole Kidman, Leslie Lowe (obscured), and Sydney Pollack on the set of Victor Ziegler's Christmas party.

Following pages: "Playing with dynamite." Tom Cruise and Nicole Kidman lay themselves bare.

Good vs. Right

It's hard to love Cruise's character, Dr. Bill Harford. He's closed off and slippery, a cipher whose choices don't make consistent sense. What personal history screenwriter Raphael had included in the original drafts—Harford's strained relationship with his father, his guilt over his prurient interest in female anatomy—Kubrick had purged from the script, leaving Cruise to play a shallow voyager who serves only to lead the audience on an odyssey of sexual temptation. Also on the page but deleted from the final film is Bill's explanatory voice-over that invited the audience to understand his feelings. Worse, Kubrick deliberately shunned including the Tom Cruise charisma fans expected in his performance, raising the question of why he cast Cruise at all. Why ask the biggest star in the world to carry your film and then hide his face under a mask for twenty minutes?

Though this is a story of sexual frustration—an emotion Cruise had played with conviction in *Born on the Fourth of July*—and jealousy, which is just the darker twin of Cruise's signature competitive streak, his performance in *Eyes Wide Shut* feels flat. He'd done vulnerability better in *Jerry Maguire* and had captured neutered paralysis a decade and a half before in *Risky Business*. Yet in nearly all of *Eyes Wide Shut*'s key emotional moments—his wife confessing to her

first and second psychological "betrayals," his patient's daughter professing her love over her father's corpse, nearly kissing a call girl's corpse in the morgue, being unmasked at the orgy—Cruise's face is stiff and visibly unfeeling, almost as if he never took the mask off at all.

Cruise's blankness makes *Eyes Wide Shut* take on an element of kabuki theater, the art form where emotional perception—not projection—is key. The whole film feels like an exercise in theatricality, as though Dr. Bill is not a person but a prop. This isn't a movie about a human possessed with distrust and jealousy—it's a movie about distrust and jealousy that simply uses a human as its conduit. With Cruise hidden in a mask and robe, the intention is to hide his individuality in the service of a larger ritualistic machine. Even in his scene with the impossibly sweet prostitute played by Vinessa Shaw, their conversation about how much cash for which physical acts doesn't spark with lust but limps along, as though the characters themselves are merely performers recognizing that this is the negotiation that is supposed to take place. "Do you suppose we should talk about money?" he asks. It's as if their whole conversation is in air quotes.

To critique Tom Cruise's performance in *Eyes Wide Shut*, it's important to distinguish between good and right. Measured against any of his previous screen roles, his acting reads as terrible. It's artificial, distant, and unrelatable. However,

the terribleness of his performance translates into a tricky logic puzzle. Onscreen, we're given only one take of the ninety-five attempts that Cruise shot. If Kubrick was a perfectionist who demanded Cruise repeat himself ninety-five times on the set, and in the editing room rejected ninety-four of those takes, then the "terrible" take Kubrick chose must be the take that Kubrick wanted. What feels flat to the audience must have felt correct to the director, so even though it's hard to appreciate Cruise's performance, at least one person must have thought the chosen take was perfect: Stanley Kubrick. And for Cruise, a perfectionist himself, who was determined to make his master happy, we're forced to defend the "badness" of his performance by recognizing him as an excellent soldier following orders.

Yet critics under the sway of thinking that the great Kubrick could do no wrong and Cruise, the popcorn hero, could do little right, blamed the actor for the director's choices and groaned that "Our forever boyish star just can't deliver."[223] The irony, however, is that in forty-five years of filmmaking, Kubrick had never asked his actors to deliver. His films had earned Oscar nominations for their acting only twice: Peter Sellers in *Dr. Strangelove* (1964) and Peter Ustinov in *Spartacus* (1960). In his much shorter career, Cruise himself had earned as many Oscar nods. That fact alone speaks to the limited value the director placed on acting. To

Kubrick, his cast was merely a tool for his vision and individual performances subservient to his intimidating authorial style. Kubrick's disinterest in actors is evident even in *Eyes Wide Shut*'s credits, which despite including two directors (Pollack and Fields) and two great character actors (Alan Cumming and Rade Serbedzija) filled the rest of its cast with new faces and tenth-billed TV actors. As much as Cruise wanted *Eyes Wide Shut* to prove, yet again, that he could act, Kubrick clearly had scant interest in giving him the opportunity.

In minor moments, Cruise's commitment to craft sneaks through. As ever, the key elements to focus on are his eyes and physical movements, which he uses to show his disinterest in his wife without ever having to say it aloud. In his very first scene, Cruise walks through his house looking for his wallet—which proves to be a key object in the film—and finally stops in front of the mirror with his back to his wife. When Kidman asks how she looks, he responds "Perfect, looks great," while pointedly not glancing at her face. He's focused on his own appearance, restlessly straightening his coat, adjusting his lapels, and fixing his cuffs. His apathy toward his wife visibly continues through the entire sequence at Victor Ziegler's Christmas party. Cruise enters, dragging her passively behind him by the hand, and though he touches her proprietorially during introductions, he

Tom Cruise imported Nicole Kidman from Australia before they even met. He'd seen the young actress fight for her life in the brutal thriller *Dead Calm* (1989) and asked his *Days of Thunder* producers Jerry Bruckheimer and Don Simpson to fly her to Hollywood for an audition. (After *Top Gun*, they owed him a favor.) Yet Kidman's role in *Days of Thunder* did the ambitious former teen TV star no favors. Just twenty-two, she was miscast as America's best neurosurgeon, and her character's romantic arc with Cruise's race car–driving hothead was pure fiction. But in reality, the couple clicked. They married six months after the movie premiered, and the next year Kidman won a Golden Globe nomination for a small part in *Billy Bathgate* (1991). Still, to Hollywood, she was simply Mrs. Tom Cruise—

more valuable in the tabloids than onscreen. Their second spouse act, *Far and Away*, again cast Kidman as the sophisticate and Cruise as the cash-chasing brute. Her temperamental Irish heiress battles his blue-collar boxer to a draw, but the film was an expensive flop. In 1995, Kidman finally found her footing: a high-profile love-interest part in *Batman Forever* gave her box office clout, while the black comedy *To Die For* won her critical respect.

By *Eyes Wide Shut*, the couple's screen image and public image had merged: she was class; he was pop. Kubrick treated them accordingly, paying her only a third of Cruise's $20 million salary, but building up her artistic ego. "He said that Tom was a roller coaster and I was a thoroughbred," Kidman confessed.[f] In his chase for credibility, Cruise was now second to his wife.

After their divorce, even serious-minded film writers like David Thomson couldn't resist gossipy speculation. "I think Kubrick makes a film that whispers to Nicole, 'You are a real actor, a sexual phenomenon—and he is not,'" he wrote. "No one can see the film without inhabiting that dismay. So why should the two central players not feel it themselves?"[g]

patronizingly pats her back like a puppy. Later when they share a romantic slow dance, he stares over her shoulder at the crowd, at the band, at anywhere but his wife's eyes. Despite their polite affection, it's unsurprising that she downs a glass of champagne the second he's out of sight.

Yet Cruise's Dr. Bill is eager to make eye contact with everyone else: Victor, Nick Nightingale, the two models at the party, and even the passed-out naked girl in the upstairs bathroom. (He underscores it in his stream-of-consciousness monologue as he attempts to revive her: "Open your eyes, look at me, look at me, look at me, look at me, look at me, Mandy.") Even so, in his body language, we see the difference between looking and seeing. He looks at the girl, but he refuses to really see her—he doesn't blink at the shock of her nude body and ignores her breasts even as he puts his face just a foot from hers. His dismissal of nudity is a pattern. The next day at his office, his very first patient is another topless, sexy woman who he treats with the same dispassion. That night when Alice accuses him of getting turned on by his patients, we're aligned with his indignation—we've seen firsthand that he's telling the truth.

His job is no accident. Kubrick's own father was a doctor, as was the father of *Traumnovelle* author Arthur Schnitzler. Both saw Dr. Bill's professional disinterest in nudity as the key to the character's problems. "The repression of normal responses to women neutralizes a person," articulated cowriter Raphael. "By renouncing those responses to females, he deadens himself."[224] Yet Cruise seems miscast in the role of a doctor, not because he lacks the obvious intelligence—he had, after all, played a Harvard-educated lawyer *twice*, in *The Firm* and *A Few Good Men*—but because on a deeper level, Dr. Bill himself barely seems to care about healing people. Over the course of the film, we see him with several patients and two corpses, and never does he appear knowledgeable and competent. He lacks the vocabulary of a doctor—compared to his legal roles, his jargon is nonexistent—and all we ever see him do is uselessly touch and prod.

Dr. Bill doesn't care about medicine because of his patients. He cares because of his status. Throughout the film, he insists on flashing his New York State medical board credentials to people who couldn't possibly care—a waitress, a costume store owner—and it's his profession that's gained him entry to Victor's exclusive party, which starts off the film. When he glances across the ballroom and spots Nightingale, a former classmate now reduced to playing the piano for cash, Cruise makes it clear his character is a snob. Listen to the downbeat finality in how he ends the sentence "He dropped out," as though Nightingale has dropped out not just of medical school but of proper society. In tune with Kubrick's demand to flatten Dr. Bill

to nothingness, Cruise introduces a new speech style: a condescending monotone that he uses in every interaction with a patient and, gratingly, during the wrong moments with his wife. In their first argument, his modulated diagnosis "This pot is making you aggressive" is a key factor in triggering her rage. It almost reads as if she recognizes from his subtle vocal cue that, like with his female subjects, he's stopped responding to her as a human.

Capitalist Power

Unquestionably, Kubrick films are never as surface level as they seem. In *Eyes Wide Shut*, the surface is a story about jealousy and desire. Yet a recitation of the events argues otherwise. Bill is surrounded by offers of sex, but acts on none. Though he's kissed by three women—the prostitute Domino (Vinessa Shaw), the grieving daughter Marion (Marie Richardson), and the mysterious woman in the mask—Cruise's lips never even push back against theirs. So why then is he determined to crash the erotic party, even at the costly expense of the taxi ride and costume? Because Dr. Bill's interest isn't in sex. It's in proving that he belongs in this rarefied, invite-only world—or that, at the very least, he can fit in. As he was in the buildup to *Interview with the Vampire*, Cruise was criticized for his lack of sexual jolt, but again that's not what either film is about. Like *Interview*, *Eyes Wide Shut* is about power. Not even sexual power—capitalist power. And capitalist power is Cruise's continual, career-long theme.

Using that lens, Cruise's performance as the repressive Dr. Bill almost makes sense. Cruise keeps the qualities that made him a star—his smile, his assurance, his chemistry—hidden under Dr. Bill's mask until the conversation turns to money or status. In only three scenes is the character allowed to be confident and charming—in the jazz club, the costume store, and the taxi cab—and in each one, the circumstances are the same: he wants a favor and can afford a bribe. Dr. Bill is alive only when he flaunts his power. Though the turning point of the plot is Alice's lustful revelation about the naval officer, which turns Bill from a homebody who drinks beer and watches football into an all-hours roamer of the streets, the turning point of Cruise's performance is the moment Nick tells him about the exclusive party—a party even more exclusive than the Ziegler's posh holiday soirée—and insists that Dr. Bill wouldn't be welcome.

Dr. Bill isn't turned on by the orgy—he's stricken by the knowledge that even as a rich, successful, handsome young doctor, he still has more social ladders to climb. This scene is the first time in the film that Cruise is active, not reactive—even with the two flirtatious models at the first party, he allowed himself to be passively

Nicole Kidman and Tom Cruise in their first film together, Tony Scott's *Days of Thunder* (1990).

109

dragged around by both elbows. Assuming all he needs are confidence and cash, Cruise spends the middle stretch of the film flaunting both: sweet-talking Nick into giving him the party's password, bribing the costume salesman to rent him a cloak after-hours, and wheedling the cabdriver into driving him $75 out of town. To underscore his cavalier wealth, he even rips a $100 bill in half. And when the orgy uncovers him as a fraud, he's aghast. Later, when he and Ziegler lay their cards on the table, his first question isn't about the dead woman or the sex— it's how they knew he didn't fit in.

Finally, his restless, taciturn pursuit of "sex" makes sense. But if we've paid attention to Cruise, we've known this from his very first words. Cruise enters the film looking for his wallet—and as we'll see through the film, his wallet is where he keeps the three things he holds most dear: his money, his medical board credentials, and his self-esteem. The line isn't in the original script. Who knows who, when, or which take added this casual clue to *Eyes Wide Shut*'s opening scene. But as Cruise would suffer most of the negative critical blowback upon the film's release, it feels only charitable to also credit him with some of the good choices in this intense merging of man, actor, and director.

Cruise made himself vulnerable before Kubrick and his devotees, but instead of being rewarded for his emotional and financial

sacrifice, he found his performance dismissed by audiences as callow. He couldn't even ask his by-then dead-and-buried director for support. *Eyes Wide Shut*'s fallout wasn't flattering: he was blamed for the film's failure, and the tabloids took a savage interest in his marriage, which would last only two more years. Yet Cruise continues to defend his two years of hard work. "I didn't like playing Dr. Bill. I didn't like him. It was unpleasant,"[225] admitted Cruise a year later in the only public criticism he's ever given. "But I would have absolutely kicked myself if I hadn't done this."[226]

7

Frank "T.J." Mackey

Magnolia (1999)
Paul Thomas Anderson

"It's not just about picking up chicks and sticking your cock in. It's about finding out what you can be in this world."
—Frank "T.J." Mackey

In England, Tom Cruise had time to kill. One evening, he and Nicole watched *Boogie Nights* (1997), the second feature from twenty-seven-year-old wunderkind Paul Thomas Anderson, a writer-director and LA native son who had become the upstart of Hollywood after his first film, *Hard Eight* (1996), made a splash at Sundance. Cruise was struck by a bungled, drug-addled robbery scene set to "Jessie's Girl" and called Anderson up with his congratulations. Anderson happened to be in London, and he gladly accepted Cruise's invitation to visit the *Eyes Wide Shut* set. Noting Kubrick's scant film crew, Anderson asked the director if he always worked on such a small scale. "How many do you need?" replied Kubrick. "I'm an asshole, man," said the humbled young auteur, "I spend too much money."[227] But he was about to embark on the most star-studded and narratively complex film of his career.

Earlier that year, Anderson's father, Ernie, had died of cancer. A late-night horror movie host who went by the name of "Ghoulardi," Mr. Anderson purchased a Betamax video camera for his son when the boy was twelve, launching the director on his path. Cruise understood. He, too, had lost his father early. But in truth he'd lost his dad—and namesake—Thomas Cruise Mapother III years before. After his parents divorced when Cruise was twelve, he'd seen his father only twice: at fifteen when his dad took him to the drive-in and on his deathbed. The elder Mapother never watched one of his son's films.

"He tried going out to see *Risky Business*, but he was in too much pain," said Cruise. In the first leg of his career, he was remarkably open about their relationship, as though the wounds were still so raw that it helped to say them aloud. "I hadn't seen my father for a number of years. I heard he was dying, and I didn't know where he was. He didn't want to be contacted. He left and didn't want to be contacted for *years*. I think he was tired of inflicting so much pain on other people that he just had to get away."[228]

"I spent some time with him. We talked," he continued. "I think he made so many mistakes that it ate him alive. Even when I went to see him, he didn't want to discuss what had occurred in the past. I said, 'Whatever you want, Dad.' But I held his hand. And I told him I loved him, and that I was going to miss him. He said when he got out of the hospital we'd go have a steak and a beer and talk about it then. He died before we could do that."[229]

His father did have time to give a few quotes to journalists who tracked him down. In 1983, he told a reporter that he had "made a personal decision to respect my son's wishes, which was for me to stay the hell out of everything," saying that they had gone over four years without communication ("a long time, at least to me") until Tom and his sisters had come by his hospital after a cancer operation. When it was suggested to the elder Mapother that their visit had meant more than words could express, he began to weep. "A lot more, a lot more."[230]

Given where the two men were at that stage of their lives—Cruise undergoing Kubrick's emotionally taxing two-year test and Anderson confronting his own father's death—it's likely they talked about their shared pasts. The evidence: when Cruise asked Anderson to write a part for him, his standard request when he met a new talent he liked, the filmmaker flew back to Los Angeles and turned up six months later with the part of Frank "T.J." Mackey, a bitter stage performer who has a wrenching meltdown beside his dying father, Big Earl.

Well, not quite. Anderson's original script was more sympathetic to Frank and Big Earl than in the final cut. In Anderson's draft, the pair reconcile with the dad soothing his son: "You are not what you think you are." But when Cruise played the role, there was no spoken redemption and only a glimpse of Mackey making peace with his pain. The final film is colder, more cutting, and closer to Cruise's childhood than to Anderson's bond with his own father—it's so close, in fact, to Cruise's own life that both he and Frank Mackey had lopped off their father's surnames before becoming famous.

Cruise leaped into his three-week stint on *Magnolia* almost immediately after Kubrick said "Cut." He was in a rush to squeeze in *Mission: Impossible II* (2000) that same year—he did, after all, have his own production company to

Frank Mackey, Cruise's most aggressive performance.

think about, and it'd been starving to get him back on the big screen. Now fifteen years into his career and with an incredible run of five $100 million–plus hits in a row (*Eyes Wide Shut* wouldn't flop until months after *Magnolia* wrapped), Cruise wielded his clout as a box office titan. He had the muscle to pick the best roles and, having already worked with most of the great directors, the might to invest in Hollywood's next generation. P. T. Anderson was about to discover what Cameron Crowe had already learned: signing Tom Cruise made you the studio's best friend and gave your film more money, more time, and more trust.

Still, Anderson was Cruise's first younger director—a full eight years younger, in fact—and he knew he had to impress. Anderson created Mackey because the complex character was "un-turn-downable."[231] As he described, his philosophy when writing for actors is, "I want to be a genius to them because their opinions mean so much to me."[232] Mackey's emotional arc with his father was in place. Now it was time to figure out the rest of the character. Said Anderson with a grin, "Something about Tom prompted a certain naughtiness in me."[233] Why not make Cruise a lascivious, woman-hating horndog?

Seduce and Destroy

Audiences who felt let down by the abandoned promise of seeing Cruise as a sex-mad therapist in *Eyes Wide Shut*—the prevalent preopening rumor—had their dreams fulfilled by Cruise's first moments as Frank "T.J." Mackey. Cruise had played lotharios before—in *Cocktail*, he bedded a woman just to win a bet—but Mackey was a whole new monster. Mackey isn't just a lover. He's a wicked psychologist, albeit uncertified, and he's more interested in inflicting pain than receiving pleasure. Just think of his tagline: "Seduce and Destroy." Seduce, sure. But *destroy*?

Cruise had never been a tabloid Casanova. He'd married Mimi Rogers at twenty-four, then married Nicole Kidman within a year of his first divorce. If anything, he was continually fighting rumors that he didn't like women *enough*. He continually headed to court to defend his image. Within one short span, he filed suits against two sex therapists who claimed to have given him and Nicole lovemaking lessons, a tabloid that pronounced him impotent and sterile, a male wrestler who claimed they'd had a romantic affair, and a magazine that announced it had a videotape of the actor in a homosexual tryst. Every case was won by Cruise, settled, or dismissed. If Cruise's sexuality had a reputation, it was that you spoke about it at your own peril.

The irony of Cruise's Mackey is that it's both his most sexual performance and one where he doesn't even lay a hand on a woman. For all of Mackey's swagger that he can make any babe

his "sex-starved servant," Anderson never shows the man in action. Anderson and Cruise actually filmed several video reenactments of Mackey bedding women—outtakes from his instructional guide—but cut them from the final product. Even fictionally within the film, we never see Cruise make good on his threat to "master the muffin," which strengthens the idea that Mackey isn't the smooth-talker he claims. Is it all bluff? Or does Mackey really believe his own hype?

Cruise is allowed scenes with only two women, and one of them is over the phone. In both, the women control *him*. His off-screen assistant, Janet, genuinely cares about his well-being. She's protective of his privacy, peppering his father's nurse (Philip Seymour Hoffman) with questions to prove his credibility, yet also tender when telling Mackey the news about his dying father. But even she—a woman paid to do Mackey's will—doesn't take his orders. When Mackey shouts, "Do your fucking job!" she refuses to be cowed. Instead, she hollers back, "I am doing my fucking job!"

Mackey's centerpiece male-versus-female showdown is another losing battle against television reporter Gwenovier (April Grace), who initially throws him—and us—off guard by acting submissive. Their interview is a teasing, fire-stoking combination where both he and she use flirtation as a tool. He wants to charm her and her camera; she wants to coo and smile until he drops his guard. Their dynamic is the distillation of every stereotype in the battle of the sexes: men using blunt chemistry to exert their power and women pretending to be impressed until they're ready to wrest control.

Cruise gives the role a fascinating combination of confidence and insecurity. He comes on like a gorilla—literally—stripping down naked in front of Gwenovier and beating his chest. The nudity was Anderson's idea. Cruise hadn't flashed his underwear since *Risky Business*, and hadn't gone fully nude since *All the Right Moves*. (The glimpse of his pubic hair has since been edited out of *Moves*.) On the day of the shoot, Cruise started the scene simply sans shirt, exposure he was used to. Then Anderson asked him to take off his pants. "I said, '*What?*'" recalled Cruise. "He said, 'Yeah, yeah, yeah. It'll be funny.'"[234] To Anderson's glee, Cruise disrobed. Gushed the director, "He's like, 'What do you want me to do, do you want me to stand on my head, do you want me to do backflips? I'll do it, I'll do anything you want.'"[235]

With his manhood a tabloid fixation, all eyes were on his crotch. And the bulge in his briefs was distractingly large. Given Anderson's previous use of a prosthetic penis in *Boogie Nights*, the columnist Michael Musto of the *Village Voice* launched a crusade to find out if "the garden hose is 100 percent real meat."[236] "I don't know whether to be insulted or feel complimented,"[237] joked Cruise, while Anderson was more definitive:

Mackey is locked in a permanent battle of the sexes (here, on the phone to his female assistant).

"Tom Cruise is the biggest movie star in the world. Are you kidding? Of course he's got the world's biggest cock."[238] (Naturally, Cruise looked into a lawsuit against Musto.)

In just three minutes, the opening act of the interview establishes, then upends, Mackey and Gwenovier's dynamic. Cruise starts the scene in full physical command. Defiantly pants-less, he rolls into a backflip—as Anderson asked—caps it with a strikingly graceful handstand, bounds into a chair, and starts panting like a dog in heat while blurting out nonsense: "Terrorists! Babes! Beauties!" Meanwhile, Gwenovier sits immobile with her back to the camera waiting for him to settle down. When Anderson finally cuts from Mackey's face to hers, we realize that this woman isn't under his spell—though he's certain she is.

Suddenly, Mackey's frantic ego-thumping seems naïve. Whether we're excited or anxious to see her dismantle him depends on how much Cruise has made us empathize against our will with this sad, show-off child. To hint at Mackey's eagerness to impress, Cruise exaggerates his movements, leaning so far forward in his chair that his skeleton looks apt to pop out of his skin. In response, Gwenovier purrs, "Calm down, take it easy, and be a good boy." She talks to him like a naughty little child, and he cheerfully responds. "Yes, ma'am!" he chirps, buttoning his shirt as though he expects her to be proud of his fingers for moving so fast. Mackey mistakes her interest

for flirting—which, in fairness, is probably part of her plan. Uncharmed, she subtly asserts her control by telling him that he missed a button.

Mackey's immature need to impress isn't written in the script, but it's there between the lines. Like Cruise's, Mackey's father abandoned the family when he was a child. Like Cruise's, Mackey's father never called. Unlike Cruise, Mackey had to watch his mother die of cancer by his fourteenth birthday. He's never grown past the pain—and in fact, underneath his adult braggadocio, Cruise clues us in that he's never grown up at all. Playing Mackey with a teenager's horny obedience speaks to his suspended adolescence—you see in him the age at which his maturity stopped. By giving us a glimpse of the broken boy inside, Cruise makes it impossible to hate Mackey, despite his unconscionable attitudes toward women. We wouldn't let the rogue near our own daughters, but we believe that he, too, needs love—despite claiming he only cares about lust.

Cruise's vulnerability is key to making *Magnolia* work. Without it, his sobbing scene at his dad's deathbed would fill us with *schadenfreude*, not sadness. It also explains why with Gwenovier he's determined to hide the truth of his origins lest she and her audience learn his secret pain. To assert Mackey's feigned authority over Gwenovier—especially when her interview gets too personal—Cruise keeps his dialogue clipped and sharp, as though withholding his

charm were punishment for her intrusiveness. He cuts off her questions by insisting that they're a waste of her time and tries to shut her down with his restless disinterest—or, failing that, derail her with sexual innuendos. But look closely and Cruise transmits Mackey's fear: his crow's-feet quiver, he bites his lips, he nods overzealously, he glances over his shoulder at his assistant for backup. Gwenovier also sees through—or ignores—his alarm. Despite his lingering, clueless confidence that he can maintain control of the conversation, their interplay is like a river overpowering a dam: she gently flows past his obstructions.

Edit out the rest of *Magnolia* to allow the interview scene to play in real time, and the shift in Cruise is even more obvious. Just minutes after his exuberant backflips, her questions have hemmed him in so tightly that he can barely move. When he realizes Gwenovier already knows the truth about his childhood, Cruise takes us through an arc of angry resignation while barely appearing to react at all—Mackey wouldn't want to give this woman the satisfaction. He doesn't even blink. All he'll allow is a change in his mouth, gradually collapsing from a grin to a forced smile to a pursed frown, which he holds, as stony as a sphinx. ("There are a lot of silent parts because I've always loved Tom Cruise silent," said Anderson. "He's a really good starer."[239]) He won't move, so Anderson does, pushing the camera so close to his face that we can see through his cold control—close enough to see him grinding his teeth. Without lifting a hand, Cruise creates a crackling air of violence. He doesn't even raise his voice—in fact, his voice gets quieter and more controlled—but his silent fury triples the tension. In the climax, all Cruise has to do is stand, loom over the still-seated Gwenovier, and calmly call her a bitch, and she recoils like she's been hit.

How to Fake Like You Are Nice and Caring

Anderson plays with Cruise's physical proportions throughout *Magnolia*. When first we see him onstage, as "Thus Spake Zarathustra" (a nod to his time with Kubrick?) rises on the sound track, we see him as Mackey wants to be seen: back-lit and poised like Superman. In theaters, the shot makes him appear both life-size and larger than life. In front of his champions, Mackey is a rock star—literally. Watch closely and Mackey's performance is Cruise's sharklike impersonation of Elvis Presley. Cruise doesn't walk, he swaggers—and curls his upper lip in a sexy snarl. Though Mackey was born and raised in Southern California, Cruise gives him a Mississippi twang. He doesn't say "Men!" or "No!" he says, "Men-*naaa*!" and "Noooo-*aaaa*!" and when really overheated drawls the word "sausage" out to three sweaty syllables, as in "Suck my big fat fucking saw-seg-*geah*!" (Did Cruise cut the original script line, "By the end

of May, you will know I'm not gay," because it cut too close to the rumors?) When he mimes humping a girl, his pelvis swivels dangerously enough to get him brought up on obscenity charges in Los Angeles—something that nearly happened to Elvis in 1957 when the Vice Squad accused him of getting too provocative with a stuffed animal while crooning "Hound Dog."

Cruise is a big Elvis fan—he's sung Elvis publicly on Jay Leno, privately in a karaoke session with the prime minister of Japan, and even snuck an Elvis bobblehead on the dashboard of his Bubble Ship in *Oblivion* (2013). In *Magnolia*, he's bold about the Mackey/Presley connection, continually poaching Elvis's windmilling arm swing to rally his crowd. (His swagger barely changed when Cruise played actual rock star Stacee Jaxx in *Rock of Ages* [2012], though instead of drowning in hate, he's drowning in drugs.) The crowd hoots and hollers like they're at a concert. Mackey isn't giving a motivational speech, he's giving a motivational performance.

And it's all Cruise. Anderson thought T.J. Mackey was a nerd. He first wanted to dress Mackey in golf pants and polo shirts. Cruise asked him to reconsider. "I always saw him wearing an armband," he insisted to Anderson, "those leather-wrist, masculine hero kind of things." Cruise pointed to the script for backup: Mackey likens himself to a mythic figure, a modern day Batman and Superman. "I was just *on* it with the character," said Cruise. "And Paul trusted that."[240] Convinced, Anderson allowed Cruise to transform the character from a cruel geek to a strutting, vest-wearing rock star. He's even visibly vain—when the spotlights hit Mackey's face, they highlight lavender circles of makeup under his eyes.

The golf pants had come from T.J. Mackey's real-world inspiration: seduction Svengali Ross Jeffries, a former paralegal. (Which might be why men trusted him—in reality, wouldn't Mackey's paying fans wonder if his pickup secret was, well, looking like Tom Cruise?) Jeffries's seminar series launched the pickup artist into the popular culture, and he took a trademark attorney along to *Magnolia* in case he had a lawsuit. "He lifted some stuff almost word for word," Jeffries complained, but ultimately decided he liked the film so much he wouldn't sue.[241] (Not that he had much of a case.)

"What Tom Cruise doesn't know is that he was playing a character that I created," explained Jeffries. "I'm not Ross Jeffries—that's a persona I put on in my seminars."[242] But Jeffries underestimates Cruise's intelligent reading of T.J. Mackey. Cruise knew that Mackey knew his act is artificial. His smooth moves have the practiced look of a performer who's done them hundreds of times in a hundred different hotel convention centers. Mackey is a self-made construct who comes to life only under the spotlight. Who naturally strides around with their arms akimbo

and fists clenched to their hips? Underscoring Mackey's control over his artificial persona, after the one-two disasters of his interview with Gwenovier and the news of father's imminent death, Cruise shows us how he switches back into character onstage as easily as putting on a mask.

However, during his final lecture ("How to fake like you are nice and caring"—ironic, as Mackey really fakes being a jerk), it's hard to tell if—or when—Mackey strays off script. "Men are shit!" he yells, "We do horrible, heinous, terrible things!" That sounds like Mackey, but Cruise's movements get crisper and angrier until the film audience alone—his in-person audience never suspects—spot the seething hate and pain. Cruise's jaw twitches, his voice builds, and when he yells, "I will not apologize for who I am," Cruise makes it deliberately hard to tell if he's talking to the crowd or himself. Mackey claims he can control a woman's mind, but can he even control his own emotions?

Cruise and Anderson couldn't figure out how to cap his mini-meltdown. "We had tried ending the scene a couple of different ways," said Cruise. With Anderson and the crew watching, the actor paced as he tried to seize upon an idea. "I went over the table on stage for a second, it was in the take, just at the end of it, and I just really wanted to throw the table," recalled Cruise. "I didn't say anything, and I didn't really make a huge move to it, but he came up to me right afterward, and he

just walked over to the table and put his hand on it and sort of tapped it a little bit as if to say, 'It's okay, let's do it.'"[243] But the masterstroke is that flipping the table doesn't end the scene. Instead, Cruise has Mackey immediately wrenching control of himself to snap back into his own character, ordering the crowd to open their white books before they clue into the emotions churning underneath his smooth surface.

Fathers and Sons

Cruise has played Mackey loud and he's played Mackey quiet. But he doesn't show us the real Mackey until he visits his dying father, played by Jason Robards. Again, Cruise added his own input to the original text and convinced Anderson to cut back on the sentiment. "In the script, it said, 'He gets to the door and he breaks down,'" noted Cruise. "And I said, 'Look, I don't feel that.'" Instead, when he gets to his parents' house, Cruise can't even be seen—he's fully blocked by the door itself. The audience hears only his voice as he falls back on the trick he tried on Gwenovier: gaining control by demanding obedience. "I want you to come in with me, and I want you to stay away from me," he orders his father's nurse, warning that he'll drop-kick the dogs if they come too close. ("I was looking for a way to make this guy human," joked Cruise. "I thought it was funny that he was afraid of dogs."[244])

Cruise insisted on playing down the sentimentality of his final scene in the movie (*see opposite*).

Opposite: An excerpt from the initial shooting script.

"I didn't know what was going to happen when I got to the house," admitted Cruise.[245] Was Mackey going to rage against his father, or crumple like a child? He does both. In a bravura single-take shot with Robards supine at the front of the frame and Hoffman, small and out of focus, watching from behind, Cruise enters the scene and stalks up to his father with exaggerated cheer. He reverts into his offensive position—the hands-on-hips macho stage pose—but Cruise lets his nerves slip: he's breathing too heavy, baring his teeth, and tapping his foot loudly just out of frame. Then the hurt rolls in like a fog. Cruise puts his superhuman body control to work. His lips purse; he shakes imperceptibly and clasps his hands together so hard that the knuckles turn white. Just as he vows, "I am not going to cry," Cruise tilts his head to the ceiling, perfectly placed so the light catches a tear seconds before it spills across his face. As he collapses into sobs, a vein pops in his forehead, his face turns painfully red, and by the time he hollers, "Don't go away, you fucking asshole!" Cruise is heaving like a hurt animal. The whole arc happens in just under two minutes, and it's arguably the best two minutes of acting in Cruise's career.

"The whole time with the character, I was skating on the edge," acknowledged Cruise.[246] The personal parallels between him and Mackey were closer than he cared to admit. In a strikingly candid 1992 interview with *GQ*, Cruise described his final moments with his father and presaged the same struggles Mackey would face seven years later. "When people can't forgive someone, my question always is, 'What have you done in your life that you can't forgive this other person?'" asked Cruise. "The things you've got to take responsibility for in your life, it makes forgiveness quite easy. And it also brought me a lot of understanding about him and the pain he was in."[247]

But by the time *Magnolia* earned him his third Academy Award nomination, Cruise had clammed up about his father. Back on the awards circuit, and this time all but certain that the Oscar was his, he wanted to build protective distance between himself and the script. And why risk voters thinking he wasn't really "acting"?

Again, Cruise lost. He'd ripped his life open for a tightly crafted, stunningly raw performance. And it still wasn't enough. Cruise was done chasing Oscars—now it was time to have fun.

How much did Tom Cruise's input change the character of Frank "T.J." Mackey? Compare two versions of Mackey's emotionally climactic scene at the bedside of his dying father Earl. Below is a transcript of Paul Thomas Anderson's original monologue:

Dad. Dad. Hey, Earl. Hey, Dad. Dad, can you wake up a minute? Dad? He's not waking up. Dad. Dad. It's me. It's Frank. It's Jack. It's Jack, Dad. I'm here. I'm here now. What do you want? Do you want anything? Just wait. Dad, do you want anything? Can you say? Oh, Dad. It's okay. Jesus. Okay. It's okay. I'm here with you now, please. I'm sorry. It's all right. Okay.

And here's the speech Cruise delivers in the final film:

You don't look that bad. You prick. "Cocksucker."

That's what you used to like to say, right? "Cocksucker." But you are a cocksucker, Earl. It hurts, doesn't it? You in a lot of pain? She was in a lot of pain. Right to the end, she was in a lot of pain. I know because I was there. You didn't like illness, though, do you? I was there. She waited for your call. For you to come. I am not going to cry. I am not going to cry for you. You cocksucker, I know you can hear me. I want you to know that I hate your fucking guts. You can just fucking die, you fuck. And I hope it hurts. I fucking hope it hurts. Why didn't you call? I fucking hate you. Goddamn you, fucking asshole. Oh, God, you fucking asshole. Don't go away, you fucking asshole. Don't go away, you fucking asshole. Oh, God, don't go away you fucking asshole.

```
298.   INT. EARL'S HOUSE - THAT MOMENT                          298.

Frank and Earl.  Earl opens his eyes a bit.

                    FRANK
               Dad...dad it's me...it's Frank...
               It's Jack....It's Jack....Dad....

Earl can barely make it but he touches Frank....Frank holds
his Dad's hand....Phil steps up closer....

                    FRANK
               I'm here.  I'm here now.  What do you want?
               Do you want anything?

                    PHIL
               I don't think, he can't...

                    FRANK
               ...just wait...Dad...you want
               something...can you say...

                    EARL
               ....fuck...fuck...fuck...

Earl is in PAIN and his hallucination make him a bit angry.

                    EARL
               ...thismssm....
```

8

Ray Ferrier

War of the Worlds (2005)
Steven Spielberg

"Where's the thunder?"
—Ray Ferrier

The only unusual thing about Tom Cruise and Steven Spielberg's rapid two-film collaboration at the turn of the millennium is that it took them so long. Both men had been at the top of their respective lists in Hollywood for decades—when they committed to making their first film together in 2001, Cruise and Spielberg had the two most solid track records in the business. Both had the power to make any film they wanted, and the dedication to make it good.

They'd known each other for years. David Geffen introduced Cruise to Spielberg during *Risky Business*, and then four years later, Spielberg agreed to direct *Rain Man*. (He had to drop out due to his previous commitment to the third Indiana Jones film.) "To me, Tom has always been like the most popular kid in school who goes out of his way to befriend the geek… me," said Spielberg. "He has a pure heart—that's been consistent about him ever since we met."[248]

Spielberg and Cruise also shared something unique—they'd survived Stanley Kubrick. While Cruise plunged into Kubrick's controlled chaos to shoot *Eyes Wide Shut*, Spielberg was also tangled up with the auteur planning *A.I. Artificial Intelligence* (2001), another one of Kubrick's several-decades-in-the-making dream projects, which he'd abandoned after accepting that technology couldn't yet build a lifelike robot boy. Spielberg's *Jurassic Park* (1993) changed his mind, and Kubrick asked the director for advice, even attempting to hand over the film in 1995. Spielberg refused. But eight months after Kubrick's death, Spielberg resolved to honor his legacy by finishing the film that Kubrick had already loosely mapped. It was a difficult, often-halted project, during which Spielberg mimicked Kubrick's obsession with secrecy, even preventing his cast from reading the complete script.

Like Cruise, Spielberg lost years forging Kubrick's vision. And, like Cruise, after fleeing Kubrick's clutches Spielberg raced to enjoy his freedom. That year, he shot a tiny uncredited cameo at a party scene in Cruise's divisive drama *Vanilla Sky* (2001). Then in 2002 alone, he released two ambitious popcorn pictures: the Leonardo DiCaprio globetrotting caper *Catch Me If You Can* and, of course, his first film with a man who understood what he'd endured, *Minority Report*, starring Tom Cruise.

From Philip K. Dick to H. G. Wells

Cruise came to Spielberg with the idea for *Minority Report* during the filming of *Eyes Wide Shut*. He'd read a half-baked adaptation of the Philip K. Dick short story and sent the director the thirty-page original. They both saw a contemporary texture in Dick's four-decade-old sci-fi thriller about a security-obsessed America that preserved peace by prosecuting people for crimes they'd yet to commit—ideas not even they knew would become much more important when the film was released in June of 2002, a year when the country's attention turned to the National Security Administration's preemptive strikes in the War on Terror. When Cruise, playing the lead cop in charge of arresting future criminals, finds himself pre-accused of killing a man he's never met, the flick becomes a slick race against time to prove his innocence that also raises questions about the value of privacy. Is what's good for humanity tolerable for the individual? What about the reverse?

Minority Report is a standard heroic adventure. Cruise is the brave rebel pressed to restore civilization's integrity, and for much of the film, he fights alone on a mission to uncover the truth. The most interesting thing about his performance is revealed in an offhand on-set anecdote. In one scene, Cruise's character must hide underwater to escape detection from a pack of small, spidery robot spies. He desperately holds his breath, but is revealed when an air bubble bursts out of his nose. Spielberg assumed the bubble would be digitally added in postproduction, but Cruise refused. He'd been practicing in his own bathtub at night for weeks and promised Spielberg he could do it himself. "I just had to figure out how to get the air and then just control my nostril," assured Cruise.[249] He did.

As expected from a partnership between two titans, *Minority Report* made its money back, although it wasn't a massive hit. Before the film's release, the two men swore to work together again. "Steven Spielberg is the greatest storyteller cinema has ever known […]," raved Cruise. "It is

Father and daughter: Tom Cruise with Dakota Fanning in *War of the Worlds* (2005).

a creative combustion."²⁵⁰ Even their processes were similar, he explained. "There's a connection and a synchronicity that finds its way into the work. To someone outside, it looks like we're not even thinking about it, but you're always thinking about it."²⁵¹

One afternoon, Cruise stopped by the set of *Catch Me If You Can* to go over the marketing for *Minority Report*. Spielberg proposed three ideas for their next project: a romance, a Western, and H. G. Wells's *The War of the Worlds*. Cruise immediately agreed to the alien invasion film—with gusto. "I just said the title, and he said, 'That's the one, that's it. That's our next project together. Go no further. Describe no more. Where do I sign?'" recalled Spielberg. "We did the pound," agreed Cruise, adding that as they smashed their fists together, "We were giggling and laughing."²⁵²

Spielberg was ecstatic. He'd wanted to remake the Wells classic for decades. At an auction in 1994, Spielberg had purchased Orson Welles's directorial script for his own infamous radio adaptation of *The War of the Worlds* for a princely $32,200—double the estimated price. Paramount studio executives were thrilled that Hollywood's box office's two biggest draws were reteaming to film a classic adventure with built-in name recognition. "No expense will be spared," boasted an unnamed exec. "Steven wants to make the film of the decade, bigger than *E.T.*"²⁵³

Yet Spielberg was in a different place from when he had made *E.T.* in 1982. So, too, was the world. Twenty years earlier in an era of relative stability, Spielberg had vowed to make films about peaceful aliens only. His classic hits like *Close Encounters of the Third Kind* (1977) argued that extraterrestrial life—and, by extension, science and the universe—was a force of neutrality, if not outright good. In his science-fiction films, even in *Minority Report*, the biggest villain mankind faces is its own fear. But the September 11th attacks, still recent during the preproduction of *War of the Worlds*, made him realize that audiences needed an outlet for a bigger, more consuming terror—one that dwarfed the stories he'd already told. "I'm more cynical in the new century than I was in the 1980s and '70s," Spielberg confessed. "It's time for me to show the dark side of space."²⁵⁴

Reconfiguring Real-Life Fears

The destruction of the World Trade Center had rattled Americans. There lingered a looming fear that even worse lay ahead—tensions similar to the previous two times *War of the Worlds* connected with an audience: the 1938 Orson Welles radio play, which preyed on the rising fears of Nazism, and the 1953 film, which dovetailed with the dawn of the Cold War. In each era, people needed to see their

Science Fiction and Scientology

In H. G. Wells's original novel, the aliens arrive on Earth in spaceships. In Steven Spielberg's adaptation, they're already on Earth—and they've been waiting to attack for aeons. Why the switch? The *Boston Phoenix*'s Gary Susman wondered if the cause might be Tom Cruise's religion, which posits that 75 million years ago, a galactic dictator named Xenu stacked our planet with extraterrestrials. So at the press conference for *War of the Worlds*, Susman asked Cruise if the film had personal resonance. The actor wasn't happy to see his promotional tour sidetracked by questions about his faith. "There's absolutely no relation to that whatsoever," insisted Cruise.[h] Of course, his denial was undermined by the fact that he erected a Scientology tent on the *War of the Worlds* set right next to where the extras took their lunch breaks. "The volunteer Scientology ministers were there to help the sick and injured," he defended to *Der Spiegel*.[i] As Cruise's career continues to veer toward sci-fi adventures like *Oblivion* and *Edge of Tomorrow* (2014)—both of which hinge on rebirth and identity, other key tenets of Scientology—these questions keep coming. But there's another question: Has the focus on his religion gone too far? After all, how frequently do journalists prod Richard Gere about his Buddhism or Ben Kingsley for being a Quaker? And how many other actors have been banned from filming in an entire country, as Tom Cruise was when Germany's Defense Ministry refused to let him shoot *Valkyrie* (2008) on location as he had "publicly professed to being a member of the Scientology cult."[j] Yet, with Cruise reportedly ranking third in the controversial church's hierarchy behind only the late L. Ron Hubbard and current chairman David Miscavige, there's a strong argument to be made that the actor is partially responsible for responding to Scientology's well-documented cases of harassment and abuse. Movie press conferences aside, Cruise is willing to participate in the public debate: "I believe in freedom of speech."[k]

fears externalized onscreen, their alarm at large and incomprehensible threats reconfigured as a cold-blooded, impassive alien genocide. "I think fear is what creates people's imagination," said Spielberg. "Primitive man—terrified of the moon, terrified of shooting meteors, frightened of the dark—painted pictures of his world inside caves."[255] As the foremost storyteller of his generation, he seemed to feel a duty to film *War of the Worlds*. "I place my admiration for Wells and his novel over my predisposition to make all aliens friendly."[256]

To fit Spielberg's vision, Cruise had to make his own extreme about-face. In *War of the Worlds*, he's the protagonist, but he's no hero. Instead of risking his own safety to save mankind as he did in *Minority Report*, Cruise's character, Ray Ferrier, saves only himself and his kids. The theme is selfishness, not sacrifice. "I said to Tom when we first started working on this project that I really wanted to make a movie where your character isn't heroic—he's running away," said Spielberg.[257] Ray doesn't fight, he hides. And he's not even a good father: he's a divorced, blue-collar jerk who barely knows his son and daughter, played by Justin Chatwin and then-relative-newcomer Dakota Fanning. The best he can do is the bare minimum: keep his children alive.

"Tom takes being a dad very seriously. So do I. So does Steven," said screenwriter David Koepp, who had also cowritten Cruise's first *Mission:*

Impossible. "That's boring. Let's talk about the times we failed hopelessly as a parent. I wanted to write a movie that's about a bad father, who's bitter, whose life had not gone where he wanted." As inspiration, Koepp reexamined Cruise's past roles. To root Ray Ferrier, he imagined a man with the Cruise cockiness but not his sense of social responsibility. Asked Koepp, "What if the guy from *Top Gun* had developed an alcohol problem and got thrown out of the military and spent the last 25 years feeling sorry for himself and ruining his personal relations?"[258]

Cruise was so eager to read Koepp's script that when the first eighty pages arrived on his forty-second birthday, he stopped celebrating and started reading. Then he immediately dialed Spielberg, who was deep into prepping his next project, *Munich* (2005), another War on Terror–themed film, based on the aftermath of the Black September attack during the 1972 Olympics in Germany. "He was actually screaming in the phone. I had to actually take the phone away from my ear, he was so excited," laughed Spielberg. The next month, Koepp mailed another fifty pages, and Cruise called Spielberg again. He had a bold proposition. "He said, 'If you move your *Munich* project, I'll move *Mission 3*,'" recalled Spielberg. Caught up in the excitement, the director agreed. "So we both decided to move our pictures back one movie, to do this immediately together."[259]

War of the Worlds was a huge undertaking. It cost $132 million, thanks both to its massive special effects budget and one of the largest extra casting calls in decades. It was the biggest job of Cruise's career—and for Spielberg, it was his fastest. With a hard opening deadline of the July Fourth weekend—only eleven months after Cruise's fateful second phone call—the pressure was on. The two leaped into preproduction that fall, wrapped shooting in spring, and completed postproduction barely in time for its visible summer holiday release.

It helped that Spielberg had essentially made this movie before. His main touchstone wasn't *E.T.* or *Close Encounters*, it was his five-Oscar-winning war movie *Saving Private Ryan* (1998). "Could I bring some of the tools I used to make *Private Ryan* to tell a real story about an intergalactic invasion of the planet Earth?" asked Spielberg.[260] In both films, the director wanted to explore the true nature of heroism and survival. Hollywood fictions insist that a hero lies within all of us. But many heroes had died in *Private Ryan*'s World War II—and others, too, would die during the collapse of the Twin Towers and the War on Terror. As seen in his brutal *Private Ryan* Normandy invasion sequence, Spielberg believed that life depends on luck—in *War of the Worlds*, the difference between life and death is as unpredictable as a screwball bullet, tumbling chunk of concrete, or listing alien laser.

Responding to 9/11

Tom Cruise—the very face of Hollywood heroism—understood what Spielberg needed to say. He, too, had been directly rattled by the attacks. Though he'd moved throughout his childhood, at his core, he was a New Yorker. His family had settled in New York in 1825 after fleeing Ireland. He was born upstate in Syracuse, graduated high school just across the river in New Jersey, and launched his career in Manhattan. When he purchased his first permanent home with his *Risky Business* paycheck, he chose a modest two bedroom, two bathroom condo in the East Village, which he owned until February of 2013. September 11th was a personal affront.

At the Academy Awards six months after the attacks, Cruise opened the show. Alone on the stage, he gave a speech designed to bridge the gap between a glossy entertainment spectacular and a country stricken with fear. "Last September came an event that would change us. An actor friend said to me, 'What are we doing? Is it important? Is it even important what I do?' And what of a night like tonight? Should we celebrate the joy and magic movies bring?" asked Cruise. "Well, dare I say it? More than ever."[261] Hollywood burst into thunderous—and relieved—applause.

The next year, Cruise cofounded the controversial New York Rescue Workers

Detoxification Project, an attempt to flush out poisons like mercury, aluminum, and magnesium from the first responders who had been polluted by their efforts at Ground Zero. On CNN's *Larry King Live*, Cruise explained that the clinic was designed to cleanse these toxins from the workers' fatty tissues before they could trigger leukemia, Parkinson's, multiple sclerosis, and cancer. As proof, his clinic claimed that during their Purification Rundown, their patients had passed odd-colored bowel movements, and his technicians decorated their walls with stained towels as proof that dangerous substances were being sweated out in their saunas.[262]

"When I started this project I was in [a] position where I knew I could help. I absolutely consider it an honor and a privilege to be here to help these men and women," insisted Cruise,[263] later adding, "This project has demonstrated that recovery is not only possible, but an incontrovertible fact."[264] But the clinic had its detractors, among them the fire department's chief medical officer, Dr. Kerry Kelly, who declared, "I have trouble believing in these purple-stained towels."[265] Furthermore, the fact that several of the fireman later joined Scientology—Cruise's religion and one he strongly advocated—raised concerns that these services were actually a ruse to convert the 9/11 heroes.

Cruise and Spielberg's shared drive to comprehend September 11th found its way into

War of the Worlds. Neither was shy about the overt connection between fact and fiction. In fact, Spielberg wrote it directly into the script. "I think 9/11 reinforced everything I'm putting into *War of the Worlds* [...]," said Spielberg. "We now know what it feels like to be terrorized... And suddenly, for the first time since the Revolutionary War, certainly the first time since the Civil War, we know what it's like to have our two front teeth knocked out [...]."[266] His imagery could have come from 9/11 news footage: the crumbled buildings, the screaming survivors, the airliner splintered into fragments. And Cruise's detoxification campaign is literally onscreen. When his neighbors explode into ash around him, Cruise's Ray Ferrier stumbles home covered in gray soot from flesh and chemicals, stares hollowly at his reflection in the mirror, and gags and sobs as he tries to get clean.

War of the Worlds feels real. It doesn't just take place directly outside Manhattan—it takes place outside of a Manhattan that has already lived through the Twin Tower attacks. When Ray's daughter, Rachel—who would have been five when the airliners crashed across the Hudson—absorbs the destruction, she interprets it using the only worldview she knows. "Is it the terrorists?!" she yelps. Her older brother struggles to shake off the same conclusion. When Ray insists that these attackers came from someplace else, the boy replies, "What, you mean like Europe?"

No hero could have stopped the Al Qaeda attacks. Neither can Ray. He's no superhero in tights; he's a dockworker in a hooded sweatshirt and Yankee cap. Now forty-three, for the first time Cruise looks tired. Bags droop under his eyes, and his hair needs a trim. He's not wholly convincing as a working-class grunt—he does, after all, have his Tom Cruise smile. But Cruise tried to rough up Ray Ferrier's edges by drawing on his own cash-strapped childhood. Not only did he and Spielberg place Ray in blue-collar Bayonne, New Jersey—an oil refinery town just seven miles away from Cruise's high school in Glen Ridge—they even asked the locals to hide their aboveground pools.

"He wasn't born a movie star," insisted Spielberg to critics surprised to see Cruise play a brute who'd never heard of hummus.[267] Visually, Spielberg diminishes him further. Cruise has never been more dwarfed by his surroundings. When the first death rays claw out of the earth, Spielberg doesn't shoot the actor as one man facing a machine. He's merely one man among many, each equal in their scramble for safety. Cruise almost never holds the frame by himself. There's nearly always another person— sometimes hundreds of them—pressing in on him from all sides. Pounding on his van, trudging alongside him on the road, churning to climb aboard his ship, the extras swirl around him and crowd his space. That an alien laser hits one man and not another is happenstance. Cruise isn't faster or smarter—he's just luckier.

An Accident of Biology

Luck is great, but it's not heroism. Around Ray, we see the real heroes of the invasion: the cops and soldiers who give the orders that he follows. Their leadership and sacrifice make no impression on him—he doesn't even pause to say thank you—but it awes his son, Robbie, who sees these men in uniform, so full of purpose and courage, as a rebuke. Unlike Ray, Robbie wants to be a hero. The first time he sees soldiers trundle toward the fighting, Robbie instinctively runs to join them. Ray can't understand. "There's nothing living in that direction!" he yells uncomprehendingly.

Cruise bravely allows Spielberg to subvert the at-all-costs, risk-taking heroic image he'd cultivated since *Top Gun*. Throughout the film, *War of the Worlds* pits Robbie's full-hearted humanism against Ray's walled-off, me-first self-preservation. Robbie wants to allow strangers in their van. Ray says no. Robbie climbs up a ship's drawbridge to rescue stragglers from falling into the water. Ray stays behind and watches. Robbie sprints to join the army during a full-scale hill assault. Ray literally pins him down to the ground and orders him to stay—and when Robbie refuses, Ray allows his only son to fight

a war that he never considers joining. Like the full-on expression of Richard Dawkins's selfish gene—the theory that humans are altruistic only when it benefits themselves or their biological lineage—Cruise's Ray tries to save only his family. Around him, people drown, burn, scream, and suffer, yet he never stops running. Even when a single mother with whom Ray seems to have a flicker of a past physical relationship attaches herself to him for help, within minutes he forgets she exists. "There's three of us," he tells a shipman as he pleads for safe passage, then corrects himself. "Five! There's only five of us!" When the woman and her daughter get separated and, presumably, die, he doesn't even pause for a moment of silence.

In fact, Cruise is so hell-bent on his family's survival, we sense he'd feel few regrets about killing other humans who get in his way. He forcefully orders his mechanic friend Manny to jump in the only working van—which, technically, Ray stole from Manny's shop—yet we sense he's inviting Manny just to make amends for the theft. He nearly runs over a mother and her child, and doesn't even ask if they're okay. Only cowardice keeps him from killing. He has a gun, he has the disregard for strangers' lives—all he lacks is the courage to pull the trigger. To prove it, when filming a scene where Ray defends the van against a mob, Spielberg made Cruise hold the gun like he was terrified to use it. Cruise practiced raising the pistol slower and more hesitantly, finally adding a small hand quiver.

Ray is one of Cruise's most unlikable roles. At best, Cruise portrays Ray like he's morally neutral to human life. Regardless, the audience roots for him because of two things: he wants so badly to survive, and he's played by Tom Cruise. Sub almost any other male actor in the role, and Ray Ferrier would feel even more morally compromised. The best thing you can say about Ray is that he's not a predator—he's prey. Cruise almost seems to model the character on a white-tailed deer: Ray is alert, and he flees at the first sign of danger. When a tree bends or a puddle ripples, he has the same instinctual response: run. He's not smart, but he's perceptive, noting when no one else does that the lightning brings no thunder, that the electric storm has stopped the battery on his watch, that the birds are flying too close to the alien tripods. With a flick of his eyes, Cruise connects us to Ray—we see what he sees, and we also see that he can't quite comprehend it.

Ray might look like a hero—he does, after all, look like Tom Cruise—but it's an accident of biology. It's enough to fool Tim Robbins's conspiracy theorist, Harlan Ogilvy, who corrals Ray and Rachel into his basement lair with the pretense of giving them shelter. He's really interested in appraising Ray, assuming he'll be useful in the counterinsurgency against the

aliens. In turn, Spielberg is using Robbins's character to allude to the freedom fighters in the Middle East—the insurgents are now us. "Now we'll be the ones coming up from underground," schemes Harlan, which in a normal heroic adventure would be the right and brave thing to do. Instead, Ray looks aghast. "I've got a plan, I know what I'm doing. How about you?" Harlan hisses. "Are you going to just sit here and wait for them to come get you?" From the expression on Ray's face, it's clear Harlan isn't too far off.

Fight? Ray prefers to hide. When the aliens and their slithering, cobra-headed probe invade the basement, Harlan picks up an ax, while Ray sneaks around like a rat. Harlan is convinced he's doing the right thing—which in any other action film, he is. The audience is in the awkward position of rooting for our protagonist to do, well, nothing. Attempting to wrestle Harlan into silence, Ray is easily knocked to the ground. Even when he fights, he loses. Desperate to keep him from revealing their location, Ray commits the ultimate cowardly act: he kills an unsuspecting man.

The murder—there is no other word for it other than murder—takes place off-screen, perhaps for suspense, or perhaps so Cruise wouldn't actually be filmed killing a man in cold blood. The choice muffles the tension, but it's still shocking: here's our Top Gun killing a fellow American. And moreover, Cruise trusted Spielberg enough that he didn't insist the character explain his motivations to the audience or his horrified daughter. Still, Fanning's eyes show that Rachel clearly comprehends the monstrous act her father has committed, and it will haunt their relationship forever.

But Cruise's Ray never stops moving long enough to tell anyone how he feels. *War of the Worlds* is a big picture with big ideas that refuses to tell us what its characters think. Cruise and Spielberg shun any emotionally blunt moments. There's no sobbing at the grand waste of life, no speech about what Ray would do for his family. He doesn't even answer questions that might lead to a speech, ignoring his children as they plead for their father to make sense of the madness. Toward the end of the film, Cruise nearly stops talking altogether. His dialogue is little more than repeatedly screaming his daughter's name. Tune out the explosions, and the last act of *War of the Worlds* is a near-silent picture, with Cruise, as ever, embracing a character who expresses himself through his arms, legs, and face.

It's a tribute to Cruise's charisma that *War of the Worlds* continues to be misread as the triumph of an ordinary man against an all-oppressive supervillain. He contributes almost nothing to the destruction of the tripods. In fact, he himself never seems to know what killed them at all—the bacteriological explanation is delivered by the narrator whose omniscience reinforces Ray's lack of importance.

We get no victorious moment from Cruise. In his last scene, Ray discovers that his entire family—two children, an ex-wife, her new husband, and his in-laws (played by Ann Robinson and Gene Barry, the stars of the 1953 film)—has survived the alien apocalypse. Any other star would have wanted to play their reunion as an emotional climax. Not Cruise. Instead, he doesn't say a word. He simply hugs his daughter, hugs his son, and stands outside his former in-laws' house until they close the door and leave Ray where he started: alone.

Loneliness masquerading as a happy ending.

9

Les Grossman

Tropic Thunder (2008)
Ben Stiller

"You know how you handle an actor? They whine about anything, you pull down their pants and you spank their ass."
—Les Grossman

In the summer of 2005, Tom Cruise's career was at a crossroads. With *War of the Worlds*, he'd just earned his biggest box office haul of all time—a number that still stands today—yet the industry buzzed with gossip that after twenty-two years on top, his reign was over.

Celebrity had changed. In 1983, Cruise's biggest image problem was distancing himself from Rob Lowe and Emilio Estevez's Brat Pack. ("Putting me in there is absolutely absurd and it pisses me off," he grumbled.[268]) He didn't see himself as the launch of Hollywood's new guard, and he definitely never saw himself as a heartthrob or tabloid fixture. Cruise wanted his success to follow the path of Hollywood legends Paul Newman and Robert Redford, stars able to balance fame and personal freedom. No one realized then that he'd be the last of the popular-but-private leading men. When gossip magazines began to intrude in the nineties, Cruise fought back. He was infamous for suing editors who published false accusations about his sex life, then donating the settlements to charity. When Princess Diana died in a car crash in Paris after being chased by photographers, he attended her funeral and spoke out loudly against reckless paparazzi culture.

The continual crusades were tough, but he battled them all. "It is the last recourse against those that published vicious lies about me and my family," Cruise declared on the footsteps of courthouse after winning a suit against England's *Empire* magazine. "I have to protect them."[269] But with the rising dominance of the Internet, instead of two-dozen major tabloids, Cruise found himself fighting a hydra of gossip blogs that spread misinformation faster than he could file lawsuits. Worse, fan culture had changed. Once, audiences were happy to hoist their favorite stars on pedestals—now they wanted to drag celebrities down to mortal level, delighting in pictures of the rich and famous shopping in sweatpants or being dragged drunken and red-faced from a bar.

Some stars were canny enough to give the press enough of an inside glimpse to continue living in peace—say, Brad Pitt and Angelina Jolie, who tidily sold the rights to the first photographs of their daughter Shiloh to *People* magazine for $4.1 million, then gave the proceeds to a Namibian charity. Cruise, however, had never played along. His work was public; his life was his own. Since the beginning of his career, he'd cautiously doled out his biography to interviewers under the pretense of intimacy, but they were the same details in every piece: his estranged father, his uprooted childhood, his poverty, his dyslexia. His adult life was locked safely away. Even when his divorce from Nicole Kidman dominated the grocery store magazine racks, he released just one quote: "Nic knows what she did."[270] Cruise refused further comment, and starved for gossip, the story suffocated. Six months later when rumors surfaced that Cruise was dating Penélope Cruz, his Spanish costar in *Vanilla Sky*, the papers had so little to report that they entertained themselves writing puns about the couple's homophone surnames.

Part of what protected Cruise was his publicist Pat Kingsley, a pit bull who required journalists to contractually promise Team Cruise's approval of the final product. When Roger Ebert railed against Kingsley's techniques in the *Chicago Sun-Times*, she relented—for him. But most cowed reporters played along. In the fourteen years Kingsley guided Cruise's image, he stayed on top while his peers publicly stumbled: Sean Penn punched the press, Rob Lowe seduced an underage girl, Robert Downey Jr. checked in and out of rehab clinics, Charlie Sheen became the face of drugs and decadence. Yet in 2004, Cruise did something surprising: he fired her. The decision was costly.

Creative Suicide

The next summer when Cruise began his publicity tour for *War of the Worlds*, he and his new flack (and sister), Lee Anne DeVette, were totally unprepared for TMZ, Perez Hilton, and the terrifyingly mean-spirited new world of celebrity journalism. They screwed up. Miscalculating this new fan fixation on "real" lives, Cruise finally decided to open up to the press—way up. On *Oprah*, he professed his love for his girlfriend of one month, the sixteen-years-younger TV actress

Tom Cruise loses the hair, begs for big hands to reinvent himself as *Tropic Thunder*'s Les Grossman.

Publicist Pat Kingsley (left, with Cruise and Kidman at the 1999 premiere of *Eyes Wide Shut*) represented Cruise from 1990 to 2004.

Opposite: Cruise on *The Tonight Show* in June 2005.

Katie Holmes. He was so excited about possibly proposing to a near-stranger that on national television, he pumped his fists, dropped to his knees, and hollered, "I can't be cool! I can't be laid-back!" If he had been a seventeen-year-old, he'd have been teased. That he was a forty-three-year-old with a public semirecent divorce sounded alarm bells, as did what was interpreted as his backhanded insult to Kidman: "I honestly haven't had this kind of feeling before."[271]

If Cruise was hoping to fit into the zeitgeist by inviting fans into his intimate life, he misjudged the mark by miles. Instead, he came across as so human that he seemed inhuman. For decades, people had clamored for drops of personal information. Now they were doused with a bucketful, and they were agape with shock—and maybe *schadenfreude*. Whether or not Cruise's rapid romance was real, that he'd trumpeted it so publicly, or really, even trumpeted it at all, made it feel false. Fans had known—or felt like they'd known—Cruise and Holmes since he was nineteen and she was twenty, which saddled the couple's love story with separate preconceived opinions about each of them. By contrast, when Cruise had first romanced Kidman and Cruz, both had the benefit of being then-relatively unknown international starlets, and his first wife, Mimi Rogers, was barely famous herself.

Three days later, Cruise went on *Access Hollywood* and questioned Brooke Shields's decision to go on the mood-enhancer Paxil while suffering postpartum depression. This caused an outrage for three reasons: first, his medical information was founded on Scientology, a religion that triggers a sometimes-deserved knee-jerk negativity. Second, he was a man questioning a woman about her cure for a condition he's biologically unable to experience. Third, his criticisms shifted from concerned to condescending. "Where has her career gone?" he asked host Billy Bush, a rhetorical jab made even more uncharitable given that it was *Endless Love*, a Brooke Shields movie, that gave Cruise his first break.[272] Four weeks later, Cruise attempted to publicly apologize on the *Today Show* with Matt Lauer. "I really care about Brooke Shields," he insisted, and he was probably being truthful. But he refused to concede that using antidepressants—as eleven percent of the American population does—was okay. "You don't know the history of psychiatry," he lectured Lauer. "I do."[273] Viewers bristled. In a thirty-three-day talk show spree from Oprah on May 23, 2005 to Lauer on June 25, 2005, Cruise incinerated over two decades of goodwill.

This recounting may smack of the tabloids, but it's the key turning point in Cruise's adult career. His public image will forever be divided into pre- and post-2005. It's impossible to analyze the career choices he's made since without acknowledging the grounds on which he made

➡️ **Media Circuses On and Off the Set**

Talk about life imitating art! Five years before the Oprah Winfrey debacle, Paul Thomas Anderson's *Magnolia* presaged Tom Cruise's PR disaster by pitting him against another female interviewer who patiently watches him talk himself into a trap. Wrote critic David Thomson upon the film's release, "You feel like you're looking at an actor staring dead-on into a mirror"—words that would prove truer than people realized at the time.[1] And *Magnolia* isn't the only parallel between Cruise's tabloid struggles and his fictional creations. In *Rock of Ages*, Cruise again plays a celebrity led astray by a lady journalist. Like Mackey—and, arguably, like Cruise himself—hair metal star Stacee Jaxx expects to control the conversation when he sits down with reporter Constance Sack (Malin Akerman). He gives

her five minutes and the middle finger; she gives him the critical drubbing of his career. It hurts. Admits Jaxx, all that matters is "people's projections of what they want me to be," a truism that's valid for any bold-faced name, be they an MTV legend, a swaggering self-help guru, or the biggest box-office star in the world. From the start of his career, Cruise was cautious toward the media. In celebrity profiles, he maintained a consistent public persona: earnest and outgoing without ceding an inch on his privacy. The details he willingly divulged— his dyslexia, his difficult childhood—were all in the past. As for his present, the answers remained the same: he loved his current movie, he loved his current lady, and he worked hard to satisfy both. It worked. That is, until Cruise got too honest. After his *Tropic*

Thunder bounce, it's understandable that Cruise would be drawn to play another comic character that sifts through his own past scandals. And hey, *Rock of Ages* even gives him a happier ending. Jaxx not only wins back the reporter's favor, he marries her.

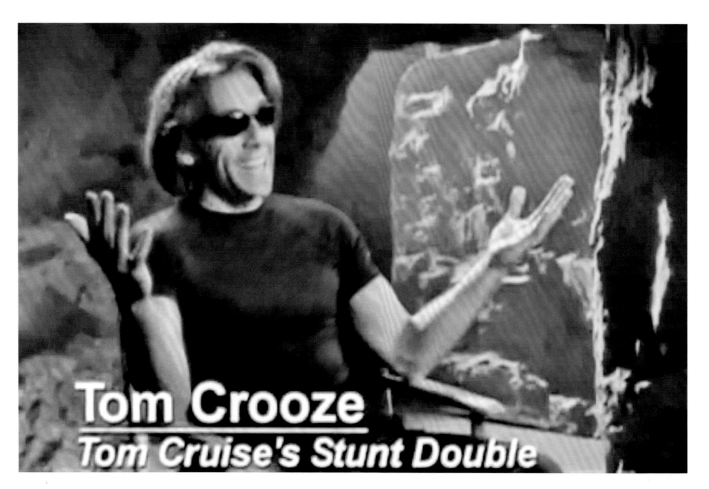

Tom Crooze
Tom Cruise's Stunt Double

Ben Stiller and Tom Cruise in *Mission: Improbable*, a skit that was broadcast at the 2000 MTV Movie Awards.

them. Pre-2005, he was an undeniable superstar forever trying to prove his talent. Post-2005, he had to prove both. Though Cruise clammed up after the Lauer interview and *War of the Worlds*—the film he'd gone on the show to promote—would open four days later to the biggest debut of his career, the damage was done. To industry pundits, the real story was that Cruise was now box office poison, even if his $64.8 million opening weekend said he wasn't.

By then, the actor had already thrown himself into *Mission: Impossible III* (2006), but his once-close collaborators were keeping their distance—even Spielberg. Despite getting two of his top-five highest openers from the actor, the director who once described working with Cruise as "one of the greatest gifts I've ever been given by this business"[274] has yet to hire him again. For the next eleven months, Cruise attempted to lie low—or as low as he could, given the tabloids' presumptive interest in his engagement to Katie Holmes and their new baby, Suri. But when *M:I:III* opened to "just" $47.7 million dollars, the fifth-biggest opening of his career (yet a harbinger of the fact that the threequel would earn $80 million less than its predecessor), Paramount chairman Sumner Redstone seized the moment as an excuse to drive a wedge between the studio and their image-troubled top earner, whose production company with Paula Wagner had been housed on its lot since 1992.

Paramount's deal with Cruise/Wagner productions cost the studio roughly $10 million a year. But its investment reaped dividends. Cruise had made the studio more money than any other actor had for any other studio. In the first six years of the millennium alone, Cruise's movies accounted for thirty-two percent of Paramount's total revenue, and tallying a collaboration that stretched all the way back to *Top Gun*, he'd made them over $2.5 billion. Though Cruise had earned his public rebuke—his positive Q Score, a measure of his popularity, had dropped from thirty percent to nineteen percent, while his negative score had doubled—even the press was struck by the studio's rapid disloyalty and the harsh words that pushed him out the door.

"His recent conduct has not been acceptable to Paramount," groused Redstone, who openly estimated that Cruise's talk show fiasco had cost *M:I:III* between $100 and $150 million. "It's nothing to do with his acting ability, he's a terrific actor. But we don't think that someone who effectuates creative suicide and costs the company revenue should be on the lot."[275]

Paula Wagner fought back. "It is graceless. It is undignified. It's not businesslike," she growled to the papers in response to Redstone's remarks. "I ask, what is his real agenda? What is he trying to do? Is this how you treat artists? If I were another actor or filmmaker, would I work at a studio that takes one of their greatest assets and

publicly does this?"[276] But Tom Cruise kept quiet. His silence in part came because he'd learned the hard way that nothing good came when he spoke his mind. Yet, even though Cruise found little funny about the public fascination with his sex life and religion, he at least knew how to laugh at himself—and he knew that it was time to let other people laugh, too.

Luckily, there was a comedian who'd been making fun of him for twenty years: Ben Stiller.

Mission: Improbable

In 1987, Stiller was a theater actor and unknown whose sole onscreen credit was one episode of *Kate & Allie* (1984–1989). That year, he cowrote and codirected his first short film, a five-minute spoof of *The Color of Money*. In Stiller's version, *The Hustler of Money*, he tears into the Tom Cruise role to play a hothead bowler who swaggers, juggles pins, and frustrates his mentor (John Mahoney of TV's *Frasier* [1993–2004], and Stiller's then-costar on Broadway) en route to compete in the Passaic, New Jersey, 9-Pin Classic. (Tagline: "Because sometimes two big stars, a famous director, and a lot of cash just isn't enough.") The spoof launched Stiller's career. *Saturday Night Live* aired his short and then two years later invited him to join their staff as a featured performer.

Stiller lasted only four episodes, but he'd been officially deemed "cool." After he directed two more shorts, MTV offered Stiller his own eponymous show in 1992, which lasted one season before getting canceled and moving over to Fox. Again, he sought comedic inspiration from Tom Cruise. In one skit, Stiller imagined Cruise launching his own greatest hits show on Broadway called *Tom Cruise: Dress Casual*, during which he interrupts his own one-man rendition of *Rain Man* to say thank you to the audience. Then he impersonated him a third time for the sketch, *A Few Good Scouts*. "Your scouts follow orders or people get wedgies!" barks Stiller's Tom Cruise, before turning to the camera and gushing about his Oscar chances. "I think I got a pretty good shot here—this is pretty intense stuff."

In 2000, Stiller resurrected his parody again for the MTV Movie Awards in a skit called *Mission: Improbable*, where he played the most inessential man in Hollywood: Tom Cruise's stunt double, Tom Crooz. "In order to do my job, I have to ask myself, 'Who is Tom Cruise? What is Tom Cruise? Why is Tom Cruise? When is Tom Cruise?'" said Stiller, which, given his fixation, wasn't that far from the truth. But what distinguished *Mission: Improbable* from the rest of Stiller's Cruise riffs was that this time Cruise joined in the joke. "He's harmless, he's harmless, he's harmless," assures Cruise, willingly playing the straight man in a sketch about himself. "He has influenced my career in some shape or form."

Opposite: Grossman videoconferences with his screw-up director (Steve Coogan).

Cruise's almost imperceptible nods and authoritative eye contact made his character a commanding presence.

Following pages: Tom Cruise came up with Les Grossman's lumbering hip-hop choreography.

That, too, was a joke that would prove to be true. In 2005, Stiller was on top of the world. It had been just over a decade since he directed his first feature, *Reality Bites* (1994), which he filmed after the final cancellation of his TV show, and the eleven years since had been great: five comedies that grossed over $100 million each, while even his smaller movies like *Zoolander* (2001), *The Royal Tenenbaums* (2001), and yes, *Reality Bites*, had made their marks on popular culture. But there was one project Stiller was still dying to make: a war movie comedy he'd dreamed up while shooting a twelfth-billed minor role in Steven Spielberg's *Empire of the Sun* (1987).

In 2006, the same year that Cruise got booted off of the Paramount lot, Stiller got his action spoof, *Tropic Thunder*, green-lit by DreamWorks Pictures, who had themselves recently been purchased by Paramount. Stiller showed his script to his by-then good friend Tom Cruise and confessed he'd been having problems figuring out what was lacking in his story about a group of unprepared actors filming a jungle survival epic they don't realize is real. Cruise had an idea. "He said, 'It's really funny, but where's the studio head? It would be really funny to see a studio head in this' […]," said Stiller, who loved Cruise's suggestion. "It solved a piece of the puzzle. It fulfilled this story point that had been bothering me for eight years."[277]

Stiller rejiggered his draft to add a new looming antagonist: studio boss Les Grossman, who terrorizes his director and gladly agrees to let one of his top actors die so he can recoup his investment with an insurance payout. It's a wickedly nasty character, so much so that Stiller initially didn't even offer the part to the man who concocted it. Instead, Stiller asked Cruise if he'd be willing to play the much kinder role of a Hollywood agent. Cruise refused—he wanted to play Grossman. And he had further demands. "He said, 'I just want to have really big hands,'" said Stiller. "I looked at him like, O.K. Really? Big hands. O.K., Tom."[278]

Shut the Fuck Up and Let Me Do My Job

The timing couldn't have been more satirically appropriate. Here was Cruise agreeing to play the ultimate foulmouthed, backstabbing studio boss just one year after Sumner Redstone's dismissal—and he was doing it with a film that was under Paramount's own banner. "The several hundred Hollywood agents, managers, publicists and reporters at the screening on the Paramount lot here couldn't have missed the joke,"[279] observed the *New York Times* after an early screening of *Tropic Thunder*. Stiller was quick to deny the connection, insisting—fruitlessly—that the Grossman role "was never going for somebody specific."[280] Yet he

also embraced the controversy. "The studio-head character, I don't know how much we're exaggerating there," joked Stiller.[281]

Visually, Stiller distanced Grossman from Redstone. Grossman is short, bald, fur-chested, and almost uncomfortably Semitic. Redstone is a lanky six-footer with copper hair and apple cheeks. (However, his original last name is the German-Jewish Rothstein.) It took Cruise and Stiller four makeup tests to find the right look. As promised, the costumers swelled Cruise's hands. Then they masked his hairline and blotched his skin, padded his stomach and ass with a rim of fat, and filled the low-V of his button-up with curly brown chest hair. During one filmed makeup test, Cruise impulsively started to hip-hop dance. Music wasn't playing. With no sound track but the general hum of noise from the crew, he began to goof off for the cameras with zero self-consciousness.

"I said, 'Keeping doing that, that's funny,' and he just went with it," laughed Stiller. "He started doing these crazy hip-hop moves that he just knows. I don't know how he knows them."[282] Cruise definitely didn't poach them from the then-eighty-five-year-old Redstone. In the original test footage, Cruise humps and swivels, thrusting his crotch and spanking the air. He'd done these moves before in *Magnolia*, but now imagining himself as a lumbering studio boss and not a laser-focused motivational speaker, Cruise blunted his choreography. His Grossman is clumsy and lumbering, his hips and arms on different rhythms as Cruise instantly clues us in that his character is so convinced he's cool that he's cluelessly ridiculous. It's the dance of someone impervious to mockery— or so powerful that no one dares mock him openly—and it's at once consciously "hip" and unconsciously silly. And Cruise clearly loves his new false hands, casually but adamantly ensuring that they looked as big as his head by keeping them close to the camera.

"We were so excited by how funny and weird it was," said Stiller with a grin.[283] He took the tape back to his office and reedited it to a rap song. Cruise thought the video was hysterical, and gave Stiller the green light not only to add a dance scene to *Tropic Thunder* but also to work a second solo shimmy into the ending credits.

The performance is fearless. Grossman's swearing and dancing grabs the attention, but it's in the quieter pauses that we see Cruise's physical command of the character: his hunched shoulders, his tightly curled lips, and the authoritative eye contact he uses to dominate a room. Grossman is so in command that not only does he make his lackey (Bill Hader) answer his cellphone, but he doesn't even have to ask him to do it. Instead, Hader stares at his face for ten seconds waiting for the go-ahead, which Cruise gives in an almost imperceptible nod. Sure, Grossman screams

expletives—he's a major reason why the comedy is rated R for "pervasive language including sexual references." But acting against the expected, Cruise delivers half of his lines with an offhand ennui. When he growls, "Why don't you get the hell out of here before I snap your dick off and jam it into your ass?" he's not angry, he's bored—he's been at this for so long, his rage no longer shocks himself. Even after Cruise allows Grossman to slam down the phone after yelling, "I am talking scorched earth, motherfucker. I will massacre you. I will *fuck you up*," he deftly undercuts his rampage by neutrally asking, "Could you find out who that was?"

On set Cruise freely improvised, and many of his spur-of-the-moment additions were left in the final cut: a crotch grab here, a whisper there, and the line, "We don't negotiate with terrorists." He helped Stiller with other script beats, telling him anecdotes about his own war-movie past and allowing one good joke at Ron Kovic, the author of *Born on the Fourth of July*. Here, Nick Nolte plays a disabled Vietnam veteran who wrote the memoir that inspired the film-with-the-film *Tropic Thunder*. In the middle of Grossman's first tirade against his screw-up director (Brit comedian Steve Coogan), the wounded vet interrupts the studio boss to speechify about fear. For a second, we respect Nolte for bravely silencing Grossman's fury. Cruise even allows Grossman to look impressed. Then Grossman calmly says, "Oh. You're a great American. This nation owes you a huge debt. Now shut the fuck up and let me do my job." Stiller and Cruise swore to keep Les Grossman a secret. Cruise's name was left off the trailers, posters, and press notes, and when a paparazzi photo of him in costume leaked in the newspapers, his lawyers immediately demanded it be taken down. "We had at least four calls from publicists and two legal letters on Friday," a celebrity rag griped to the press.[284] Cruise might have enjoyed exerting his authority over the gossip mags, but he really just wanted the role to be a surprise, a sneaky reminder to audiences that twenty-seven years into his career, they had yet to figure him out. And publicity-wise, the secrecy was a boost. Said DreamWorks spokesman Chip Sullivan, "Because we purposefully didn't include Tom Cruise in any of the marketing materials, his performance is definitely getting attention."[285]

In fact, it was possible for audiences to finish *Tropic Thunder* before they even realized it was Tom Cruise at all. "Some people totally get it off the bat," said Stiller, "and then other people don't know till the end."[286] For the first time in his career, Cruise had hidden his involvement and he'd hidden his face. Even though he'd gladly worn masks in *Vanilla Sky*, *Mission: Impossible*, and *Eyes Wide Shut*, the films had faithfully allowed him to take them off to reassure fans that, yes, he was still handsome Tom Cruise. That *Tropic Thunder* had buried the presence of

Tom Cruise refused to let his name slip in the promotional material and allowed it only in the end credits.

SCREENPLAY BY

JUSTIN THEROUX & BEN STILLER
* AND *
ETAN COHEN

MUSIC SUPERVISOR
* GEORGE *
DRAKOULIAS

AND TOM
CRUISE
AS LES GROSSMAN

what had been, until recently, the most surefire hitmaker in Hollywood testifies to how far he and Hollywood assumed he'd fallen—and what risks he was willing to take to claw back on top.

Interestingly, people assume that Cruise had to be convinced to take on the career-resurrecting role of Les Grossman. The truth is, without Tom Cruise, Les Grossman wouldn't exist. He brainstormed the character, shaped his look, and even added the dancing that made him infamous. Admitted Stiller, "His whole thing in the movie really just developed organically from a lot of his ideas."[287]

A Talent for Comedy

Cruise is strikingly good at pure comedy. *Risky Business* and *Jerry Maguire* were dramas couched in humor, but Les Grossman's sole purpose is laughs. (Still, what unites the three is that Cruise plays each part deadpan, knowing that the humor comes more from his presence than anything he'll actually say.) Grossman doesn't have to find himself, and he definitely doesn't learn a lesson—he exists solely to entertain. The only time Cruise had attempted anything similar was a straight-faced cameo in 2002's *Austin Powers in Goldmember,* where he had a two-line role as "Austin Powers," the lead role in the film within-a-film that opens the movie. (The fake film's fake director: Steven Spielberg.)

Cruise's avoidance of comedy roles is mysterious: they make money and they earn goodwill, and he's proven that he's talented enough to take them on. And Cruise's performance roots were in comedy and musicals. As a child, he'd entertain his family when they couldn't afford the movies. "I'd create different characters and ad-lib sketches to make my sisters and my mother feel better. I'd try to make them laugh. I'd do Donald Duck as John Wayne. I'd watch *Soul Train* and imitate the dancers. […] I guess you can say that's where it started," recalled Cruise. Even when he found fame shooting Hollywood dramas, he continued to lean on those early living room skits. "I wanted the audience to be happy just like I wanted to make my sisters and my mother happy when I did those skits as a kid."[288]

In fact, it was a stage performance of the musical comedy *Guys and Dolls* that hooked Cruise on acting. But though he's largely steered clear of showcasing his skills on film—besides the disastrously received *Rock of Ages*, in which his Stacee Jaxx was, at least, the sole bright spot— you can see his background even in his dramatic roles as Cruise's athletic, detailed command over his body recalls the confident grace of Gene Kelly. Sure, it takes talent to tap dance, but it also takes talent to dance deliberately badly.

Heartened by the applause for Les Grossman, Cruise vowed he'd love to shoot more comedies.

He even reportedly attached his name to two: *The Hardy Men*, a kids' book update intended to costar Stiller, and a comedy about a New York chef forced to waste his talents at a school cafeteria. Yet neither project has come to fruition. Perhaps he thinks a leading comedic role is too much of a risk?

Instead, Cruise seems eager only to rehash Les Grossman. Two summers after *Tropic Thunder* hit theaters—a lifetime in pop culture years—Cruise resurrected the character at the MTV Movie Awards, bringing his creative relationship with Ben Stiller nearly full circle. The bit was a test balloon to see if fans seriously wanted a Les Grossman spin-off feature. Since then, scripts have reportedly been drafted and presumably discarded—even as this book goes to print, there are still rumblings of Grossman's return. But it feels like Cruise is again misinterpreting his twenty-first-century fans. What audiences loved about Les Grossman was that Cruise had giddily gotten weird. Repeating the character—i.e., playing it safe—would be a mistake. But maybe Cruise knows best: he has, after all, made over $2 billion dollars playing the same character four times.

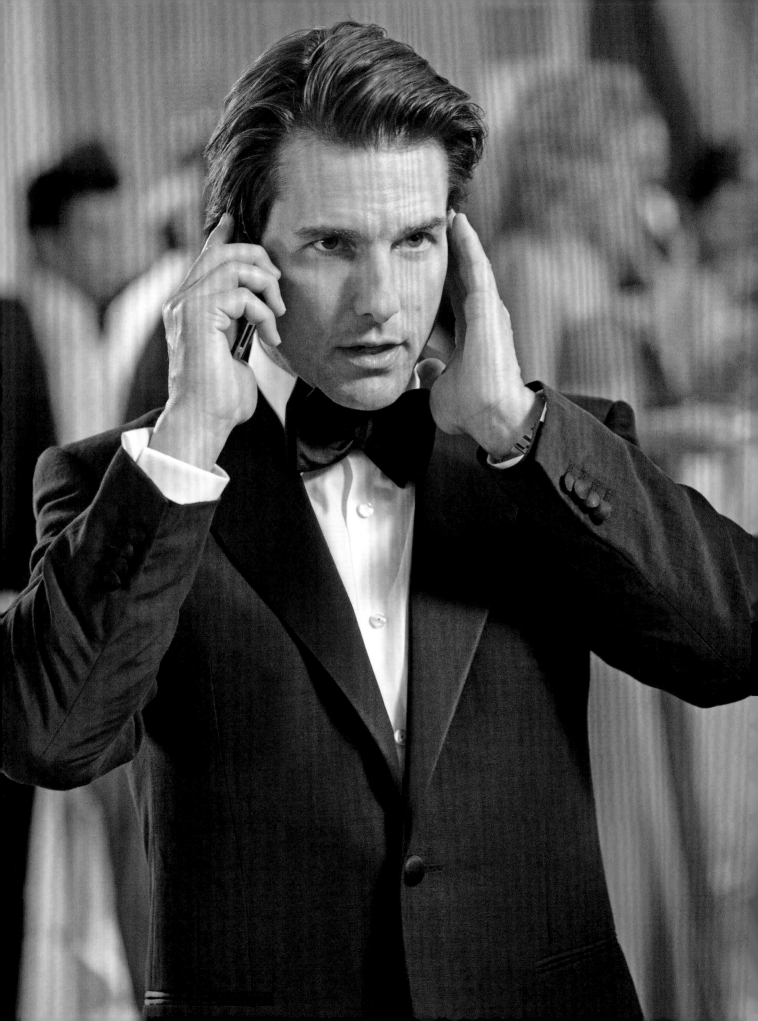

10

Ethan Hunt

Mission: Impossible — Ghost Protocol (2011)
Brad Bird

"Mission accomplished! No! *No!*"
—Ethan Hunt

Mission: Impossible is Tom Cruise's everything—both good and bad. It's the first film he produced, his first franchise, and his first action role. When the series soars, Tom Cruise is a hero. When it underperforms, Tom Cruise is to blame. During the fifteen-year stretch from 1996 to 2011 in which Cruise shot four *Mission: Impossible* films, he's been the audience's only constant. The directors have changed, the costars have changed, and the missions are, of course, always different and always impossible. Even his character, Ethan Hunt, has changed. By the final film, he bears so little resemblance to his first appearance that there's arguably no such person as Ethan Hunt at all. He's merely a cipher who gives the actor an excuse to get physical. To start at the first *Mission: Impossible* and finish at the last is to watch Tom Cruise—more so than Cruise's supposed character—grow old and weary, while still getting the job done. No one watches a *Mission: Impossible* movie and thinks, "Look at Ethan Hunt leaping over a car!" They think, "Look at Tom Cruise!"

After four films—and with a fifth all but certain—Tom Cruise is so tied to *Mission: Impossible* that it's important to remember that these are exactly the films he didn't want to do. For the first ten years of his career, Cruise refused to do sequels. He even refused to do an action movie. In his twenties and thirties, Cruise shunned a fortune by turning down *Top Gun 2* to do dramas. He even chose projects that were sequel-proof: *Rain Man 2*? *Born of the Fourth of July 2*? *A Few Good Men 2*? And when a character still struck enough of a chord that producers and audiences begged him to return, say as Lestat in *Interview with the Vampire*, Cruise said no.

Even more striking was his adamance against being a hero who holds a gun, perhaps a holdout from his temporary typecasting after playing a machine-gunning lunatic in *Taps*. While *Top Gun* has the air of an action movie, Maverick never throws a punch or points a pistol—all the actual work is done by his plane. Ditto for *Days of Thunder*, another marvel of machinery. Mitch McDeere in *The Firm* has guns pointed at him, but remains a soft Harvard-educated lawyer. He can't throw a punch—all he can do is think and run.

Tom Cruise could have spent his career acting in adult dramas. But by 1996, two things had changed: his job title and the industry itself. Hollywood had regressed. Just eight years early, a mature story like *Rain Man* had had the clout to be the top film of 1988. In 1996, it was *Independence Day*. Audiences weren't packing theaters to see Oscar winners. They wanted thrills and explosions. If Cruise wanted to remain on top, he had to get with the times. And he had a second motivation to pick a popcorn project: he was now a producer. Cruise/Wagner Productions, his company with longtime agent Paula Wagner, was hungry to make its reputation. While his heart might belong to intelligent dramas, first he needed to give his company's bank accounts a hit. Cruise needed a film that would let him do both.

"I'd been offered a lot of different kinds of action movies, but nothing really interested me," admitted Cruise. "I thought I'd seen it before."[289] Already continually struggling against his callow image, he didn't want to play just another violent meathead. He'd seen how *Rambo* both solidified and kneecapped Sylvester Stallone's fortunes. Ideally, Cruise would find a property that highlighted bravery *and* brains, and eventually he seized upon one: a TV show that had launched the year he entered first grade.

From TV to the Silver Screen

Mission: Impossible ran for seven seasons on CBS from 1966 to 1973. Even in its time, its adventures were unusually nonviolent—a key point if Cruise wanted to keep his flick a family-friendly PG-13. In the Impossible Mission Force's efforts to eliminate evil foreign powers or domestic crime bosses, the team rarely hoisted a gun. Instead, they relied on invention and machinations—costumes, gadgets, and trickery—as their tools. The IMF didn't need to be the heroes. They were happy merely to passive-aggressively finagle ways for their enemies to be assassinated by their own people or, even more passively, to trick the wicked into taping a confession that could be used against them in a court of law.

Ethan Hunt, Cruise's only franchise character ... for now.

The property was unexpected, underestimated, and perfect for Cruise. *Mission: Impossible* had been briefly rebooted in 1988 during a writers' strike, as ABC could shoot old, already-written episodes for cheap. It had minor name brand recognition among the younger generation, but was also unlikely to involve Cruise/Wagner in an expensive bidding war. In one of his first producer meetings with Paramount, Cruise made his pitch.

"I was talking to Sherry Lansing and I said, 'Who's got *Mission: Impossible*?'" he recalled. "They said, 'We have *Mission: Impossible*!' And I said, 'Great! I would like to make that into a movie.'" The studio was on board, but Cruise was surprised to have to defend his decision. "People looked at me a little cross-eyed because it was a TV series and at that time people weren't really doing that," he said. Indeed, he arguably (and regrettably) triggered a flood of imitators as Hollywood would later reboot every TV show from *The Flintstones* (1994) to *Bewitched* (2005) to *Get Smart* (2008). But Cruise was convincing. "It's a big canvas and it lent itself to characters who use their wits to overcome situations," he described, "and I thought we'd get a nice ensemble cast together and have a lot of fun.'"[290]

Though Cruise jokingly grumbled that producing was a "thankless job," he was a natural. As an actor, he'd never just memorized his lines, showed up, and thought only of his part of the film. He'd always thought of the big picture. From *Losin' It* onward, Cruise knew the success of the film reflected on him, and therefore he was invested in making his films successful. "The reason I produce is I just want to be a part of it," he explained, adding that it was a natural progression in his creative evolution. "You want to take that step into finding out, 'What kind of movies do I want to make? What kind of movies am I interested in?' You know, maybe there's not a role in it for me, but I want to *see* this movie."[291]

Cruise had logged hours on seventeen movie sets before taking the reins on *Mission: Impossible* in 1996. He'd worked with some of the best—and the most different—directors, and the prince of preparation was prepared. "I've been making movies for so long as an actor that there's a lot of shortcuts I can take, because I know how to get there," he insisted. "I could apply that to producing very quickly, and I think it helped us save a lot of money."[292] The boast wasn't empty: *Mission: Impossible* didn't just wrap on-time and on-budget—it wrapped under time and under budget, a feat for anyone, let alone a first-time producer who'd chosen to work with an intimidating auteur.

Brian De Palma was a quirky choice to direct the first *Mission: Impossible*. A critical darling early in his career, he'd made some of the most memorable movies of the seventies and eighties—*Carrie* (1976), *Dressed to Kill* (1980), *Scarface* (1983)—each a low-budget genre flick with a distinctive personality. He made brilliant trash, or trashy brilliance. But what he didn't make was money. His biggest hit to date, 1987's *The Untouchables*, made less than *Cocktail*, which in Cruise's world meant it was a disappointment. A typical Tom Cruise movie made more in its opening weekend than most of De Palma's films did over their entire run. By entrusting the veteran with the keys to his franchise, Cruise told the world he wanted quality—and that he was relying on his own stardom to make the cash.

The two didn't always get along. Cruise rode De Palma hard, forcing him to get cheap and creative even while enjoying the biggest budget of his career. But Cruise rode himself as hard. He insisted on wrapping some scenes in just two or three takes, and when he kept losing his balance while filming a one-story leap, he didn't hold up the production or beg off to be replaced with a stunt double. He put English pound coins in the soles of his shoes to better distribute his weight. Though this was De Palma's highest profile set, the director was game to act like an indie renegade, even shooting the exploding-fish-tanks-in-a-restaurant scene without a permit.

Cruise had deliberately chosen a preexisting property, but he didn't want his *Mission: Impossible* to be beholden to the original. He asked the screenwriters (who included *War of the Worlds'* David Koepp) to create new characters, preserving only the part of sixties TV show leader Jim Phelps, now nearing retirement age, and gave the part to Oscar winner Jon Voight. For himself, Cruise had Koepp concoct a new character: Ethan Hunt, the group's second-in-command. And then, so they could turn an ensemble TV show into a star project, the writers immediately killed off the rest of Hunt's team.

The Evolution of Ethan Hunt

Ethan Hunt is a Tom Cruise stereotype: leather jacket-clad, big-grinning, and cocky. He's two parts Maverick to one part *Color of Money*'s Vincent Lauria, chewing gum during meetings and telling Phelps to his face that he's "getting soft in his old age." (You can almost understand why Phelps sets Hunt up to take the fall for stolen secrets.) But Hunt is also utterly guileless—an odd trait in an international spy— as though despite the perils of his career, he's never had anything go wrong. At the start of the first film, the worst thing Hunt complains about is the coffee in Kiev. When he insists that his agency superior has "never seen me very upset," that's probably true. As Ethan Hunt learns to distrust everyone, he matures into a cynic.

By *Ghost Protocol*, Ethan Hunt has stopped smiling. Though it's tempting to argue that his somberness is the natural progression of the franchise, the truth is the franchise has never kept a steady hand on his character, or even on itself. "I always hoped that if it did work I'd be able to have a big platform for a popcorn movie and to bring in different filmmakers who could share the love of this genre and see what it is that interests us," said Cruise,[293] and when the first film worked like gangbusters—it was the third-highest grossing film of 1996 after Will Smith's aliens and *Twister*'s tornadoes—he kept his word. Every *Mission: Impossible* installment has switched directors, and in turn switched tones: the slick De Palma gives way to the slow-mo emotionality of John Woo, J.J. Abrams's cruel clockwork thriller clearing a path for Brad Bird's cartoonish hijinks. But to hire helmers he found interesting, Cruise sacrificed giving Ethan Hunt a steady arc.

In the first *Mission: Impossible*, Hunt is a focused hero who can't be bothered to woo Claire Phelps (Emmanuelle Béart). In the second, he's a goofy romantic who wastes the first thirty minutes of the film bedding Nyah (Thandie Newton)—his mission, that he vaguely bothers to accept, is less important than getting to finish the film embracing his babe in a park. (De Palma's Ethan Hunt would punch himself in the face if he ever said "Damn, you're beautiful"

as pillow talk.) In the third *Mission*, Hunt is a devoted newlywed (Nyah *who?*) desperate to keep his bride, Julia (Michelle Monaghan), safe—the film opens with him weeping, yet another new trait. By the fourth, Hunt is sexless. He's merely a pinball batted around the screen, a dervish who barely blinks at the sight of his new costar Paula Patton in a bustier. Compare the four *Mission: Impossible* films, and the only consistent things about Ethan Hunt are that he's good with his fists and he never dates blondes.

Tom Cruise himself was also in flux between the third and fourth *Mission: Impossible* films. Less than two years after throwing him off the Paramount lot, Sumner Redstone was ready to make amends—or, at least, ready to make more money from one of his studio's only solid franchises. When asked about a fourth *Mission* film during a trip to South Korea in 2008, Redstone replied, "If Paramount decides—and they will make the decision—to move ahead with him, I will not object."[294] Tom Cruise didn't immediately sign a contract, but he began to think about the series' next move. Again, he had another unusual directorial choice.

Pixar animator and director Brad Bird had helmed three of the most critically adored cartoons of the last decade: *The Iron Giant* (1999), *The Incredibles* (2004), and *Ratatouille* (2007). It was *The Incredibles*—a smart, emotional caper about a family of superheroes—

24.02 РЫБА ПИЛА

KOSMOS.COM

that captured Cruise's attention. He called Bird and invited him to his house. They talked about their favorite movies, and Cruise liked what he heard. "I said, 'If you ever want to direct live action, please direct me,'" recalled Cruise. "Even in his animated work, he shoots like a live action director. His sequences are amazing, as are his characters. He has great wit and sense of composition and he knows how to keep the tension and suspense in his stories."[295]

Bird had been doted upon during his time at Pixar. But that Cruise had repeatedly given his trust to different directors and their visions made Bird, in turn, trust him and his now-producer J.J. Abrams. "They don't try to get the directors to conform to the style of the franchise, which would mean just plugging yourself in and being a robot," noted Bird. "All of the films contain similar elements with Ethan Hunt addressing unsolvable problems, but each one has its own distinct flavor and style."[296] To make sure everyone was in synch with Bird's vision, Cruise even required the stunt choreographers to watch *The Incredibles* to get a sense of Bird's deadpan, physics-bending physical comedy.

Mission: Impossible—Ghost Protocol has the feel of a silent cartoon. Scrapping the first three films entirely, this Ethan Hunt isn't a greenhorn, lover boy, or fiancé—he's Wile E. Coyote: a relentless, speechless predator. In the first thirty minutes, he speaks fewer than twenty sentences, and when he does talk, it's only to say the essentials: "What?" "Where?" and "We're going into the Kremlin." Forget the action hero quip-cracking shtick. When Hunt almost runs over a herd of camels, he merely states the fact—"Camels"—and continues to drive. Even though his partner Jane (Paula Patton) has just seen her own boyfriend murdered, he keeps his feelings to himself—and he definitely doesn't ask her about hers. When she and Hunt finally broach the subject of his wife Julia's death, his big revealing speech is one sentence: "We can't get them back."

Instead, Cruise does all of Hunt's talking with his body: here, crossing his elbows and staring sternly are intelligible forms of communication that mean, respectively, "Open this door" and "No, we aren't going to kill the lady assassin." Unlike the Hunt of the first films, who thoroughly laid out how he would shimmy through a vent, block a laser alarm, and rappel into a microclimate-controlled chamber, this Hunt doesn't explain his plans. Instead, he merely makes us aware of them a moment before they happen with a flick of his eyes—just enough to let us see Ethan Hunt calculating the mental geometry of skidding down a four-story building. Cruise's slight pauses between desperation, decision, and action turn a fast stunt into a fleet roller coaster of emotion: what's-he-going-to-do-no-he-can't-be-wow-he-just-did.

But Hunt—and by extension, Cruise—says plenty by the physical punishment he takes. Cruise had always preferred to do his own stunts, everything from the perfect corner pocket shot in *The Color of Money* to the whiplash race-car driving in *Days of Thunder*. (Bragged *Thunder* producer Jerry Bruckheimer, "No vehicle is too fast for Tom, and no stunt too difficult."[297]) Cruise's athleticism was a gift, and as he got older and took on more physical roles, it became his obsession. He'd always been fearless. "When I was five years old, I'd climb the tallest tree possible, get to the top so when the wind was blowing I'd hang on as the branch swayed back and forth," he reminisced. Soon after, he'd flip off the roof into snowbanks, and by twelve, he'd saved up to buy a motorbike. Even then, four years before getting his license, Cruise didn't just cruise the bike down the street—he built ramps to jump over garbage cans. "I crashed a lot [...]," he joked, admitting he broke his nose three times. "No one thought of helmets or pads back then."[298] But Cruise never slowed down.

By 2000's *Mission: Impossible II*, Cruise was adamant about doing his own stunts, even if it meant climbing Utah's 2,000-foot-tall Dead Horse Point cliff, and, just as dangerously, hiding the truth from then-Paramount head Sherry Lansing. "I held back sending them any film until we'd finished the sequence because I love her and didn't want to give her a heart attack," he laughed.[299] Despite the insurance risk of the biggest star in the world doing some of the most dangerous stunts on film, he even steamrollered Steven Spielberg into letting him do his own wirework in *War of the Worlds*. "I don't like my actors doing stunts [...], but then Tom came in and saw that I was shooting a scene without him and immediately put on the harness," sighed Spielberg. "I have a real tough time stopping Tom Cruise."[300]

"I think it adds to the excitement for an audience," Cruise insisted.[301] His increasing adamance about doing his own stunt work runs counter to Hollywood's increasing reliance on CG effects—he's a throwback to the movies of his youth when special effects meant Charlton Heston steering his own chariot in *Ben-Hur* (1959). For *Mission: Impossible—Ghost Protocol*, Cruise's official headlining comeback picture after the Oscar striver *Lions for Lambs* (2007) tanked and the Cameron Diaz romp *Knight and Day* (2010) fizzled, he was determined to reach back into the stunts of the past to prove he was still on top of the world. Literally.

Top of the World

Dubai's 2,722-foot Burj Khalifa tower is the tallest building on earth. "Yes, it's high," noted Cruise calmly.[302] He and Bird chose the set

Playing with the tropes of traditional action movies, the aging hero can no longer outrun danger – like the Kremlin exploding.

piece first, then wrote a scene around it where Ethan Hunt is forced to rappel up the side of the skyscraper using only electric gripping gloves. And only Cruise thought he'd actually climb it. The effects team spent six months of prep assuming the final sequence would be fully done in digital, only to completely retool when they learned Cruise would actually be dangling outside the building in a harness. (If anything, it made their job harder—now they had to erase dozens of real-life wires from the tower's mirrored surface instead of simply painting in the hero.)

Everyone was worried. "I told him, 'Tom, nobody is going to know it's not you. There's no reason for you to do this," said stunt coordinator Gregg Smrz. "The producers were getting really nervous and he wanted to take it further and further." Cruise simply replied, "But I'm having *fun*."[303] Still, the actor/producer prepared for everything. Not only did he have the production staff build a replica of the top of the tower so he could practice scrambling around on the surface, he even insisted that they heat the glass up to 100 degrees—the real temperature of the exterior after baking in the Dubai sun. And when nature wasn't suspenseful enough, Cruise made his job even harder. Surprised to learn that there was little wind at the top of the tower, he requested the crew add a custom-built 120 mph wind machine so his clothes and hair would flap in the breeze.

Bird shot the sequence two thirds of the way up the building. "If I'm at the third or the second floor, a fall will kill me anyway. I might as well be on the 124th floor," rationalized Cruise, who argued that the stunt was simply the latest in a Hollywood lineage of vicarious danger, his nod to Harold Lloyd dangling from the clock or Buster Keaton standing stiffly as a real house collapsed around him. The filming took four days, included a four-story free fall that left Cruise's ribs bruised. Still, even while the cameras rolled, he paused several times to wave to the crowd below—and when shooting wrapped, he climbed another thousand feet to the very top of the spire, perching on a spot no more than three feet across, to pose smiling and barefoot for the ultimate photo op. "It's not that you don't feel fear," he explained. "It's about figuring out why and what to do with it."[304]

And that wasn't Cruise's only extreme stunt. For *Ghost Protocol*, he slid four stories down a wire and tumbled across a van, hurdled a sedan, and jumped over a prison railing with the loose confidence of Fred Astaire. But, crucially, Bird hit upon a way to humanize this older, wearier Ethan: many of his physical stunts fail. He can't outrun a sandstorm, he can't outrun a jeep, and though action heroes have been outrunning bombs since the dawn of cinema, Hunt can't even outrun the exploding Kremlin. Both he and the audience are surprised to see him wake up in a Moscow hospital, and to endear us to him even more Bird focuses on the identifiable bits of pain he suffers, the small detail of his bare feet running down a Russian sidewalk.

In previous *Mission: Impossible* films, a younger Ethan Hunt progressed through the plot as though simply checking off a series of challenges. In *Ghost Protocol*, he's forever failing and then having to switch plans to make up for his mistakes. If the Dubai sequence was about defying gravity, the climax—a tussle between him and villain Kurt Hendricks (Michael Nyqvist) for control of a briefcase—is about succumbing to it. The battering fight takes place in a shifting parking garage made entirely of metal, concrete, and glass where Cruise clangs against steel and smashes into windshields. If the grand finale of *Mission: Impossible*, in which Hunt nearly getting his neck severed by a helicopter blade, was a lucky near-miss, the grand finale of *Ghost Protocol* is the human body accepting punishment. Nearly fifty when he shot the sequence, Cruise's Ethan Hunt is fifteen years older than in the first film, and he shows every minute of it. Limping, sweaty, and gasping for air, the actor earns our respect not because his character is superhuman but because he's all too human. When Cruise's eyes bulge as he drives a car off a 100-foot plummet, it's like he's saying, "I can't believe I'm doing this either."

"He's ruined me for everyone else," said Bird. In his first live-action film, he'd gotten to direct a man who allowed his body to be treated like a cartoon. "I'm not going to understand after this point why any actor doesn't want to do all of their own stunts and hang off a mile-high building. He truly loves the movies and the movie-making process and he knows a ton about it—he's made for movies the way Michael Phelps is built for swimming."[305]

A Flat Hero

Ghost Protocol was a critical and commercial hit. Cruise was once again ascendant, and he'd earned it by self-flagellating on film. Gushed the *Village Voice*, "Like a Hindu's rejuvenating bath in the Ganges, a dip in the *Mission: Impossible* series serves to wash away perceived doubts about its star's enduring clout."[306] Added the *New York Times*' Manohla Dargis, "[W]hat you see isn't just a man doing a crazy stunt but also one poignantly denying his own mortality."[307]

But with Cruise's accolades for *Mission: Impossible—Ghost Protocol* comes the bittersweet irony of knowing it's the triumphant celebration of the career he never wanted. Cruise has spent more than three decades trying to prove he could act. In moments, he's accomplished it: three Oscar nominations, three Golden Globes wins, and the adoration of every

Cruise and director Brad Bird discuss one of the most spectacular sequences in the movie.

Following pages: Climbing Dubai's Burj Khalifa, the world's highest skyscraper.

Does Tom Cruise run? Does a fish swim? Cruise not only has the most distinctive gait in Hollywood—the *New Yorker*'s Anthony Lane drolly applauded his "ability to remain totally upright when sprinting, as if carrying an invisible egg and spoon"—he's got the most omnipresent run, with close-watchers tallying that over eighty percent of his films feature him in a mad dash.[m] He's run across soccer fields, football fields, tropical beaches, and an enchanted forest, toward proms and midterm exams and street fights and helicopters, away from missiles and more missiles and aliens and a detonated aquarium, over snowy hills, through pool halls, subways, small town Main Streets, Greenwich Village, and an abandoned Times Square, in tuxedos and Irish dungarees, and alongside everyone from soldiers to samurais. In

Mission: Impossible—Ghost Protocol alone, Cruise runs in a dust storm, he runs in traffic, and he even runs down the side of a skyscraper. Ever since 2006, when filmmaker Jeremiah Gall edited a compilation of Cruise's running called *Just Cruise* ("From way back, he has always been running," Gall told the *LA Weekly*), the actor's need for speed has become a cultural and Internet meme.[n] Actress Jessica Chastain claims he influenced her sprinting in *Zero Dark Thirty* (2012), for which she won a Best Actress Academy Award nomination, and sitcom star Courtney Cox even parodied his moves on her TV show *Cougar Town*. "You know he goes faster because he karate chops the air," she quips.[o] Asked to comment on the phenomenon, frequent Cruise impersonator Ben Stiller explained, "I think

Tom Cruise's running has a huge impact on the world. I mean, let's face it. Culturally, everybody wants to run like Tom Cruise."[p]

director he's worked with. Yet the respect hasn't
stuck. Ever since *Top Gun*, he's been written
off as a flat hero. Finally, in *Ghost Protocol*, he
played one—and people loved it. To audiences,
Ghost Protocol was just Cruise doing what he
does best. But it's also Cruise doing what he
never wanted to do, and giving up on earning
credibility with his talent in favor of earning it
with painful stunts. To win back the people's
favor, he had to forsake the career he wanted—
but at least if he sold out, he was doing it on
his own terms.

   "Here's the game I'm playing," Cruise said
with a shrug six months after *Ghost Protocol*'s
success. "I want to make great films that
entertain an audience and hold up. I can control
only the effort I put into it and the experience
we have making it. After that, it is what it is."[308]

Conclusion

"I always ask myself why I would want to do a film. What does it offer me? What do I have to offer it?"[309]
—Tom Cruise, 1986

"Once I've done something, I don't want to do it again. That just bores me," pronounced Tom Cruise two months after *Top Gun* stormed the summer on its way to becoming the biggest hit of the year.[310] He meant it. For the next nineteen years, he repeated directors—and franchises—only once, giving *Top Gun*'s Tony Scott a second crack with *Days of Thunder* and resurrecting Ethan Hunt for *Mission: Impossible II*. But after his image-upending 2005, Tom Cruise's career changed. The self-described "serious-minded actor"—the description he'd insisted on in the press notes for *Top Gun*—who'd once shunned action spectaculars would shoot five of them in the next seven years.[311] Some were hits (*Mission: Impossible III* and *Ghost Protocol*), some were misses (*Knight and Day*), and some were just happy to make back their money (*Jack Reacher* [2012], *Oblivion*). Yet collectively they rechristened Cruise as the popcorn king, in part because he still has no other competition.

It's not the career twenty-six-year-old Tom Cruise pictured when he swore, "It would be easy for me to go into a commercial movie, but I want to do something that will get me out of bed in the morning."[312] That year, his film *Rain Man* had won the Best Picture Oscar, and he'd shot his next Best Picture nominee, *Born on the Fourth of July*. The future looked limitless. And, like every ambitious actor, he wanted to direct. "Finding my own voice as a director's gonna be interesting to see," he pledged.[313] He helmed a smotheringly stylized thirty-minute episode of Showtime's noir series *Fallen Angels* in 1993. Yet Cruise still hasn't directed a feature, though he's certainly prepared. In his three decades in Hollywood, he's been an actor, producer, developer, uncredited writer, and devoted student of the set who's contributed his input in everything from costumes to stunt choreography.

Cruise is ready to take that leap. But he still has a Best Actor statuette to win. And he still has a few more great directors to work with—the Coen Brothers, Quentin Tarantino, Steven Soderbergh, Ang Lee—who could, and should,

help Cruise create the character who will finally earn him that long-overdue award, and the respect that comes with it. He's reconquered the box office and won back his audience, who arguably never really left. The actor who braved Frank "T.J." Mackey, Dr. Bill Harford, Ron Kovic, and Les Grossman has the talent and the courage. Now it's time for Tom Cruise to take another big risk. What he can't do is continue playing it safe with action heroes and franchises.

However, as this book goes to print, Tom Cruise is pursuing the film he once bravely refused: *Top Gun 2*.

Following pages: Cruise in carefully relaxed mode at Los Angeles' Union Station, in 1983.

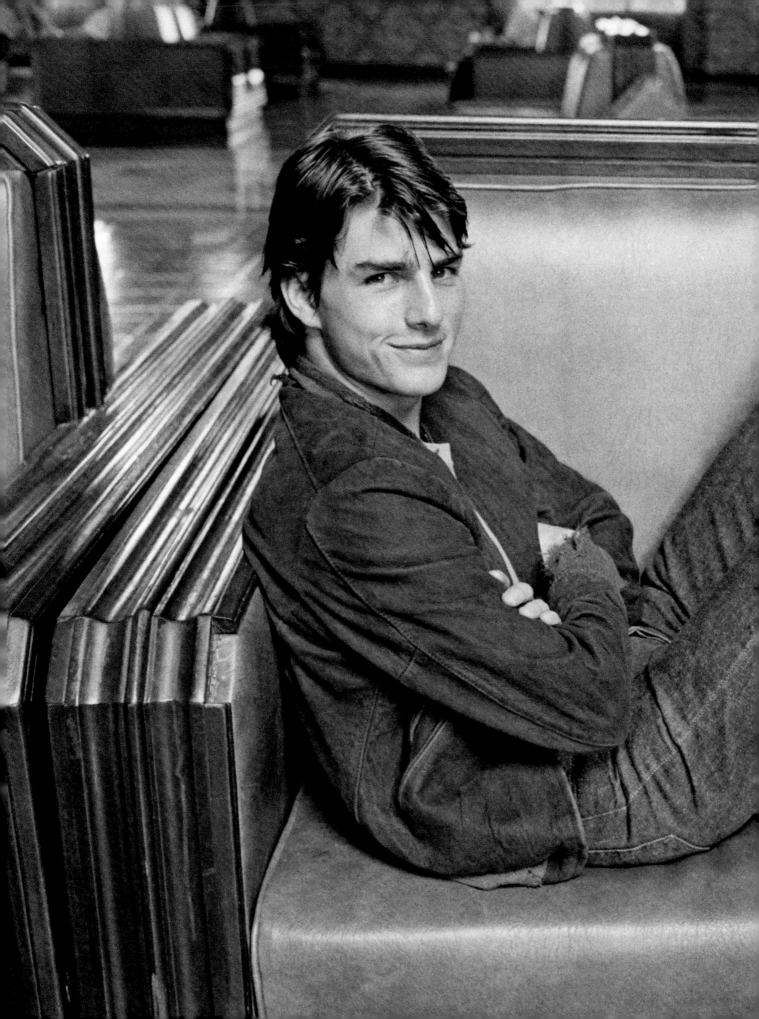

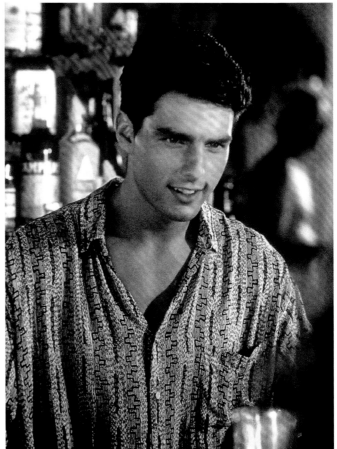

1962
Thomas Cruise Mapother IV born in Syracuse, New York.

1973
Cruise's parents divorce and his mother, Mary Lee, moves their four children from Ottawa, Canada, to Louisville, Kentucky.

1976
Enrolls in a Franciscan seminary, but decides to remain only one year.

1978
Injures his knee and is forced to abandon his dreams of earning a wrestling scholarship and a slot on the US Olympic squad. Instead, Cruise auditions for the school production of *Guys and Dolls* and wins the lead.

1980
Graduates high school and moves to Manhattan to become an actor. Shortens name to Tom Cruise and promises his family that if he doesn't succeed in ten years, he'll abandon the idea and move home.

1981
After spotting Cruise onstage in *Godspell*, director Franco Zeffirelli gives him a bit part in *Endless Love*. He has less than a minute of screen time, but parlays it into another minor role in the teen war drama *Taps* and quickly replaces the original actor hired to play the psychopathic David Shawn.

1982
Pressured to accept a star role in the sex comedy *Losin' It*. Regrets the decision and switches agents to Paula Wagner, who will guide the next two and a half decades of his career.
Pushes for a small part in Francis Ford Coppola's *The Outsiders*, then pushes even harder to play the lead in Paul Brickman's *Risky Business*.

1983
Risky Business makes Cruise a star.
Films the blue-collar football drama *All the Right Moves* and buys an apartment in New York, where he lives with his girlfriend and costar Rebecca De Mornay.

1984
Decamps to London for the grueling, effects-heavy *Legend* shoot, in which he plays a woodland sprite.

1985
Tentatively agrees to work on the script for *Top Gun*. Agrees to play the star, brash pilot Pete "Maverick" Mitchell.

1986
Top Gun is the highest-grossing blockbuster of the year. Cruise is awarded a star on the Hollywood Walk of Fame.

1987
Martin Scorsese's *The Color of Money*, for which Cruise's costar Paul Newman wins an Academy Award for

Best Actor. Cruise is not nominated.
Marries Mimi Rogers, who introduces him to Scientology.

1988
Barry Levinson's *Rain Man*, for which Cruise's costar Dustin Hoffman wins an Academy Award for Best Actor. Cruise is not nominated.
Wins a Razzie for *Cocktail*.

1989
Oliver Stone's *Born on the Fourth of July*, for which Cruise finally wins his first Academy Award nomination for Best Actor but loses to Daniel Day-Lewis for *My Left Foot*. Cruise does, however, win the Golden Globe.

1990
Divorces Mimi Rogers in February.
Marries his *Days of Thunder* costar Nicole Kidman in December.

1992
Cruise and Kidman star in the box office disappointment *Far and Away*.
They adopt their daughter, Isabella.
His career stabilizes with the critically adored *A Few Good Men*.

1993
Defies *Interview with the Vampire* author Anne Rice by refusing to resign from playing the lead role of Lestat. Stars in the financial smash *The Firm*.

Launches Cruise/Wagner Productions.

1994
Anne Rice applauds Cruise's performance in *Interview with the Vampire*.

1995
Adopts son, Connor.

1996
Cruise/Wagner kicks off the successful *Mission: Impossible* franchise.
Cruise nominated for his second Best Actor Academy Award for the title role in *Jerry Maguire*, but loses to Geoffrey Rush for *Shine*. Again settles for the Golden Globe.

1997
Cruise and Kidman move to London for Stanley Kubrick's *Eyes Wide Shut*, where they remain for the next two years.

1999
Stanley Kubrick dies. *Eyes Wide Shut* is released to middling reviews.
Cruise accepts a key role in Paul Thomas Anderson's ensemble drama *Magnolia*, and his searing turn as Frank "T.J." Mackey scores him his third Golden Globe statue and his third Academy Award nomination. This time, he loses the Oscar to Michael Caine for *The Cider House Rules*.

2000
Mission: Impossible II is a huge hit, reinforcing the concept of Cruise as a franchise action hero.

2001
Cruise files to divorce Nicole Kidman, triggering a tabloid frenzy. Begins dating his *Vanilla Sky* costar, the Spanish actress Penélope Cruz.

2002
Teams up with Steven Spielberg for *Minority Report*.

2003
Edward Zwick's ambitious but ignored *The Last Samurai* is released.

2004
Breaks up with Penélope Cruz and also his longtime publicist Pat Kingsley. "Finally" plays a villain in Michael Mann's *Collateral*, where Cruise is cast as a sharklike professional assassin.

2005
Begins dating Katie Holmes. Touts the relationship on *The Oprah Winfrey Show* and then gets into a heated debate over antidepressants on *The Today Show* with Matt Lauer.
Despite the negative fan response, *War of the Worlds* is a huge summer hit.

2006
Cruise and Holmes give birth to their daughter, Suri, in April and marry six months later. Scientology head David Miscavige serves as his best man.
Mission: Impossible III underperforms and Paramount head Sumner Redstone openly blames Cruise's public missteps, kicking Cruise/Wagner Productions off the lot. Reports circulate that Cruise's popularity, or Q Score, has fallen forty percent.

2007
Cruise's pedigreed Iraq War drama *Lions for Lambs* is

176

a critical failure, despite the involvement of Meryl Streep and Robert Redford.

2008
Disguises himself as fat and bald for a secret cameo in the Ben Stiller comedy *Tropic Thunder*, which restores some of his public goodwill. Cruise/Wagner Productions dissolves.
The German government, which openly deems Scientology a cult, creates negative publicity for Cruise's Hitler drama, *Valkyrie*.

2009
The first year without a new Cruise film since he was sequestered filming *Eyes Wide Shut*.

2010
Knight and Day, an action caper costarring Cameron Diaz, underwhelms at the US box office but makes $185.5 million abroad, solidifying Cruise's strength as a global star.

2011
Mission: Impossible—Ghost Protocol is a hit; Cruise's biggest domestic success in six years.

2012
Divorces Katie Holmes. Cruise's heavy metal musical, *Rock of Ages*, tanks, but his gruff thriller *Jack Reacher* is a modest hit.
Cruise confirms *Mission: Impossible 5*.

2013
Oblivion, a slow-burning sci-fi film, fails to connect with audiences.
Top Gun is theatrically rereleased in 3-D.

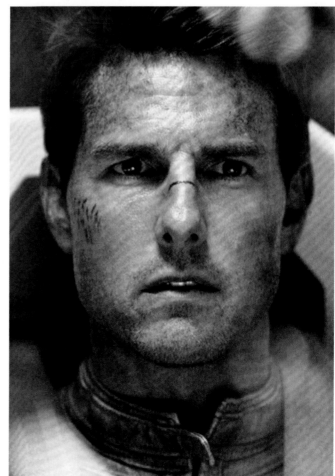

TOM CRUISE

Cocktail

Quand il remplit les verres,
il renverse les cœurs.

DUSTIN TOM
HOFFMAN CRUISE

Ils sont différents
Ils sont frères
Ils se rencontrent
pour la première fois

UN FILM DE BARRY LEVINSON

RAIN MAN

UNITED ARTISTS présente
UNE PRODUCTION GUBER-PETERS COMPANY · UN FILM DE BARRY LEVINSON
DUSTIN HOFFMAN · TOM CRUISE · RAIN MAN · VALERIA GOLINO
MUSIQUE DE HANS ZIMMER · CHEF DÉCORATEUR IDA RANDOM
DIRECTEUR DE LA PHOTOGRAPHIE JOHN SEALE, A.C.S. · CO-PRODUCTEUR GERALD R. MOLEN
PRODUCTEURS EXÉCUTIFS PETER GUBER ET JON PETERS · HISTOIRE DE BARRY MORROW
SCÉNARIO DE RONALD BASS ET BARRY MORROW · PRODUIT PAR MARK JOHNSON
RÉALISÉ PAR BARRY LEVINSON

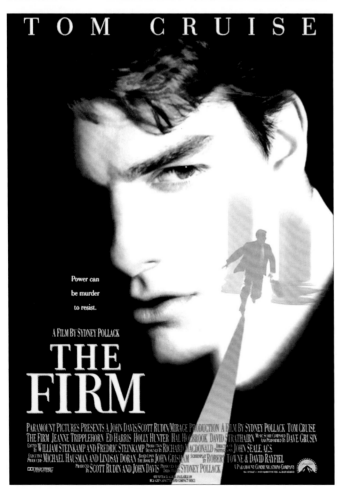

TOM CRUISE

Power can
be murder
to resist.

A FILM BY SYDNEY POLLACK

THE
FIRM

PARAMOUNT PICTURES PRESENTS A JOHN DAVIS SCOTT RUDIN/MIRAGE PRODUCTION A FILM BY SYDNEY POLLACK TOM CRUISE
THE FIRM JEANNE TRIPPLEHORN ED HARRIS HOLLY HUNTER HAL HOLBROOK DAVID STRATHAIRN MUSIC COMPOSED DAVE GRUSIN
EDITED WILLIAM STEINKAMP AND FREDRIC STEINKAMP PRODUCTION DESIGNED RICHARD MACDONALD DIRECTOR OF PHOTOGRAPHY JOHN SEALE, A.C.S.
EXECUTIVE PRODUCER MICHAEL HAUSMAN AND LINDSAY DORAN BASED UPON THE BOOK JOHN GRISHAM SCREENPLAY ROBERT TOWNE & DAVID RAYFIEL
PRODUCED B SCOTT RUDIN AND JOHN DAVIS DIRECTED SYDNEY POLLACK A PARAMOUNT COMMUNICATIONS COMPANY

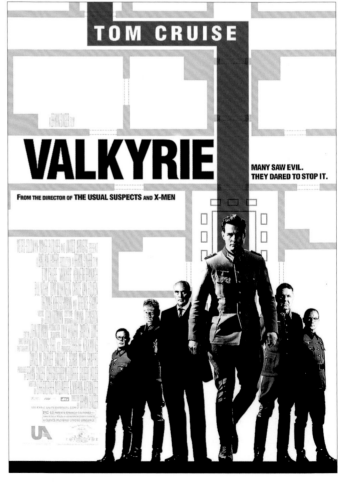

TOM CRUISE

VALKYRIE

MANY SAW EVIL.
THEY DARED TO STOP IT.

FROM THE DIRECTOR OF THE USUAL SUSPECTS AND X-MEN

1981

Endless Love

Directed by Franco Zeffirelli *Screenplay* Judith Rascoe, based on the novel by Scott Spencer *Cinematography* David Watkin *Set Decoration* Alan Hicks *Original Music* Jonathan Tunick *Film Editing* Michael J. Sheridan *Produced by* Dyson Lovell. With Brooke Shields (Jade Butterfield), Martin Hewitt (David Axelrod), Shirley Knight (Ann Butterfield), Don Murray (Hugh Butterfield), Richard Kiley (Arthur Axelrod), Beatrice Straight (Rose Axelrod), James Spader (Keith Butterfield), Ian Ziering (Sammy Butterfield), Tom Cruise (Billy).

Taps

Directed by Harold Becker *Screenplay* Robert Mark Kamen, Darryl Ponicsan, and James Lineberger, based on a novel by Devery Freeman *Cinematography* Owen Roizman *Set Decoration* Carl Biddiscombe *Original Music* Maurice Jarre *Film Editing* Maury Winetrobe *Produced by* Howard B. Jaffe and Stanley R. Jaffe. With George C. Scott (General Harlan Bache), Timothy Hutton (Cadet Major Brian Moreland), Ronny Cox (Colonel Kerby), Sean Penn (Cadet Captain Alex Dwyer), Tom Cruise (David Shawn).

1983

Losin' It

Directed by Curtis Hanson *Screenplay* Bill L. Norton *Cinematography* Gilbert Taylor *Set Decoration* Lynda Burbank *Original Music* Kenneth Wannberg *Film Editing* Richard Halsey *Produced by* Bryan Gindoff and Hannah Hempstead. With Tom Cruise (Woody), Jackie Earle Haley (Dave), John Stockwell (Spider), John P. Navin Jr. (Wendell), Shelley Long (Kathy).

The Outsiders

Directed by Francis Ford Coppola *Screenplay* Kathleen Rowell, based on the novel by S. E. Hinton *Cinematography* Stephen H. Burum *Set Decoration* Gary Fettis *Original Music* Carmine Coppola *Film Editing* Anne Goursaud *Produced by* Kim Aubry, Gray Frederickson, and Fred Roos. With C. Thomas Howell (Ponyboy Curtis), Matt Dillon (Dallas Winston), Ralph Macchio (Johnny Cade), Patrick Swayze (Darrel Curtis), Rob Lowe (Sodapop Curtis), Emilio Estevez (To-Bit Matthews), Tom Cruise (Steve Randle), Diane Lane (Cherry Valance), Tom Waits (Buck Merrill).

Risky Business

Directed by Paul Brickman *Screenplay* Paul Brickman *Cinematography* Bruce Surtees and Reynaldo Villalobos *Set Decoration* Ralph Hall *Original Music* Tangerine Dream *Film Editing* Richard Chew *Produced by* Jon Avnet and Steve Tisch. With Tom Cruise (Joel Goodsen), Rebecca De Mornay (Lana), Joe Pantoliano (Guido), Richard Masur (Rutherford), Bronson Pinchot (Barry), Curtis Armstrong (Miles), Nicholas Pryor (Joel's Father), Janey Carroll (Joel's Mother).

All the Right Moves

Directed by Michael Chapman *Screenplay* Michael Kane, based on an article by Pat Jordan *Cinematography* Jan de Bont *Set Decoration* Ernie Bishop *Original Music* David Richard Campbell *Film Editing* David Garfield *Produced by* Stephen Deutsch and Lucille Ball. With Tom Cruise (Stefen Djordjevic), Craig T. Nelson (Nickerson), Lea Thompson (Lisa), Charles Cioffi (Pop), Gary Graham (Greg), Paul Carafotes (Salvucci), Chris Penn (Brian).

1985

Legend

Directed by Ridley Scott *Screenplay* Willian Hjortsberg *Cinematography* Alex Thomson *Set Decoration* Ann Molio *Original Music* Tangerine Dream *Film Editing* Terry Rawlings *Produced by* Amon Milchan. With Tom Cruise (Jack), Mia Sara (Lili), Tim Curry (Darkness), David Bennent (Grump), Alice Playten (Blix), Billy Barty (Screwball).

1986

Top Gun

Directed by Tony Scott *Screenplay* Jim Cash and Jack Epps Jr., based on an article by Ehud Yonay *Cinematography* Jeffrey L. Kimball *Set Decoration* Robert R. Benton *Original Music* Harold Faltermeyer *Film Editing* Chris Lenenson and Billy Weber *Produced by* Jerry Bruckheimer and Don Simpson. With Tom Cruise (Maverick), Kelly McGillis (Charlie); Val Kilmer (Iceman), Anthony Edwards (Goose), Tom Skerritt (Viper), Michael Ironside (Jester), John Stockwell (Cougar), Barry Tubb (Wolfman), Rick Rossovich (Slider), Tim Robbins (Merlin), Clarence Gilyard Jr. (Sundown), Whip Hubley (Hollywood), James Tolkan (Stinger), Meg Ryan (Carole).

The Color of Money

Directed by Martin Scorsese *Screenplay* Richard Price, based on the novel by Walter Tevis *Cinematography* Michael Ballhaus *Set Decoration* Karen O'Hara *Film Editing* Thelma Schoonmaker *Produced by* Irving Axelrad and Dodie Foster. With Paul Newman (Fast Eddie Felson), Tom Cruise (Vincent Lauria), Mary Elizabeth Mastrantonio (Carmen), Helen Shaver (Janelle), John Turturro (Julian), Bill Cobbs (Orvis), Iggy Pop (Skinny Player on Road), Forest Whitaker (Amos), Bruce A. Young (Moselle).

1988

Cocktail

Directed by Roger Donaldson *Screenplay* Heywood Gould *Cinematography* Dean Semler *Set Decoration* Hilton Rosemarin *Original Music* J. Peter Robinson *Film Editing* Neil Travis *Produced by* Robert W. Cort and Ted Field. With Tom Cruise (Brian Flanagan),

Bryan Brown (Doug Coughlin), Elizabeth Shue (Jordan Mooney), Lisa Banes (Bonnie), Laurence Luckinbill (Mr. Mooney), Kelly Lynch (Kerry Coughlin), Gina Gershon (Coral), Ron Dean (Uncle Pat).

Rain Man
Directed by Barry Levinson *Screenplay* Ronald Bass and Barry Morrow *Cinematography* John Seale *Set Decoration* Linda DeScenna *Original Music* Hans Zimmer *Film Editing* Stu Linder *Produced by* Mark Johnson. With Dustin Hoffman (Raymond Babbitt), Tom Cruise (Charlie Babbitt), Valeria Golina (Susanna), Gerald R. Molen (Dr. Bruner), Jack Murdock (John Mooney), Michael D. Roberts (Vern), Bonnie Hunt (Sally Dibbs), Beth Grant (Mother at Farm House).

1989
Born on the Fourth of July
Directed by Oliver Stone *Screenplay* Oliver Stone and Ron Kovic, based on the autobiography of Ron Kovic *Cinematography* Robert Richardson *Set Decoration* Derek R. Hill *Original Music* John Williams *Film Editing* David Brenner and Joe Hutshing *Produced by* A. Kitman Ho, Lope V. Juban Jr., Oliver Stone. With Tom Cruise (Ron Kovic), Raymond J. Barry (Mr. Kovic), Caroline Kava (Mrs. Kovic), Tom Berenger (Recruiting Gunnery Sgt. Hayes), Frank Whaley (Timmy), Stephen Baldwin (Billy Vorsovich), Kyra Sedgwick (Donna), Tom Sizemore (Vet – Villa Ducle), Abbie Hoffman (Strike Organizer), Willem Dafoe (Charlie).

1990
Days of Thunder
Directed by Tony Scott *Screenplay* Robert Towne and Tom Cruise *Cinematography* Ward Russell *Set Decoration*

Thomas L. Roysden *Original Music* Hans Zimmer *Film Editing* Robert C. Jones, Chris Lebenzon, Bert Lovitt, Michael Tronick, Stuart Waks, Billy Weber *Produced by* Jerry Bruckheimer and Don Simpson. With Tom Cruise (Cole Trickle), Nicole Kidman (Dr. Claire Lewicki), Robert Duvall (Harry Hogge), Randy Quaid (Tim Daland), Cary Elwes (Russ Wheeler), Michael Rooker (Rowdy Burns), Fred Dalton Thompson (Big John), John C. Reilly (Buck Bretherton), Don Simpson (Aldo Bennedetti).

1992
Far and Away
Directed by Ron Howard *Screenplay* Bob Dolman *Cinematography* Mikael Salomon *Set Decoration* Richard C. Goddard *Original Music* John Williams *Film Editing* Daniel P. Hanley and Mike Hill *Produced by* Ron Howard. With Tom Cruise (Joseph Donnelly), Nicole Kidman (Shannon Christie), Thomas Gibson (Stephen Chase) Robert Prosky (Daniel Christie), Barbara Babcock (Nora Christie), Cyril Cusack (Danty Duff), Eileen Pollock (Molly Kay), Colm Meaney (Kelly), Jared Harris (Paddy).

A Few Good Men
Directed by Rob Reiner *Screenplay* Aaron Sorkin *Cinematography* Robert Richardson *Set Decoration* Michael Taylor *Original Music* Marc Shaiman *Film Editing* Robert Leighton and Steven Nevius *Produced by* David Brown, Rob Reiner, and Andrew Scheinman. With Tom Cruise (Lt. Daniel Kaffee), Jack Nicholson (Col. Nathan R. Jessup), Demi Moore (Lt. Cdr. JoAnne Galloway), Kevin Bacon (Capt. Jack Ross), Keifer Sutherland (Lt. Jonathan Kendrick), Kevin Pollak (Lt. Sam Weinberg), James Marshall (Pfc. Louden Downey), J.T. Walsh (Lt. Col. Matthew Andrew Markinson),

Christopher Guest (Dr. Stone), Noah Wyle (Cpl. Jeffrey Barnes), Cuba Gooding Jr. (Cpl. Carl Hammaker), Aaron Sorkin (Man in Bar).

1993
The Firm
Directed by Sydney Pollack *Screenplay* David Rabe, Robert Towne and David Rayfiel, based on the novel by John Grisham *Cinematography* John Seale *Set Decoration* Casey Hallenbeck *Original Music* David Grusin *Film Editing* Fredric Steinkamp and William Steinkamp *Produced by* John Davis, Sydney Pollack, and Scott Rudin. With Tom Cruise (Mitch McDeere), Jeanne Tripplehorn (Abby McDeere), Gene Hackman (Avery Tolar), Hal Holbrook (Oliver Lambert), Terry Kinney (Lamar Quinn), Wilford Brimley (William Devasher), Ed Harris (Wayne Tarrance), Holly Hunter (Tammy Hemphill), David Strathaim (Ray McDeere), Gary Busey (Eddie Lomax), Tobin Bell (The Nordic Man), Dean Norris (The Squat Man).

1994
Interview with the Vampire: The Vampire Chronicles
Directed by Neil Jordan *Screenplay* Anne Rice *Cinematography* Philippe Rousselot *Set Decoration* Francesca Lo Schiavo *Original Music* Elliot Goldenthal *Film Editing* Mick Audsley and Joke van Wijk *Produced by* David Geffen and Stephen Woolley. With Brad Pitt (Louis de Pointe du Lac), Christian Slater (Daniel Malloy), Tom Cruise (Lestat de Lioncourt), Thandie Newton (Yvette), Kirsten Dunst (Claudia), Stephen Rea (Santiago), Antonio Banderas (Armand).

1996
Mission: Impossible
Directed by Brian De Palma *Screenplay* David Koepp and Robert Towne

Cinematography Stephen H. Burum *Set Decoration* Peter Howitt *Original Music* Danny Elfman *Film Editing* Paul Hirsch *Produced by* Tom Cruise and Paula Wagner. With Tom Cruise (Ethan Hunt), Jon Voight (Jim Phelps), Emmanuelle Beart (Claire Phelps), Henry Czerny (Eugene Kittridge), Jean Reno (Franz Krieger), Ving Rhames (Luther Stickell), Kristen Scott Thomas (Sarah Davies), Vanessa Redgrave (Max), Dale Dye (Frank Barnes), Emilio Estevez (Jack Harmon).

1996
Jerry Maguire
Directed by Cameron Crowe *Screenplay* Cameron Crowe *Cinematography* Janusz Kaminski *Set Decoration* Clay A. Griffith *Film Editing* Joe Hutshing and David Moritz *Produced by* James L. Brooks, Cameron Crowe, Laurence Mark, and Richard Sakai. With Tom Cruise (Jerry Maguire), Cuba Gooding Jr. (Rod Tidwell), Renee Zellweger (Dorothy Boyd), Kelly Preston (Avery Bishop), Jerry O'Connell (Frank Cushman), Beau Bridges (Matt Cushman), Jay Mohr (Bob Sugar), Bonnie Hunt (Laurel Boyd), Regina King (Marcee Tidwell), Jonathan Lipnicki (Ray Boyd), Todd Louiso (Chad the Nanny), Mark Pellington (Bill Dooler), Eric Stoltz (Ethan Valhere).

1999
Eyes Wide Shut
Directed by Stanley Kubrick *Screenplay* Stanley Kubrick and Frederic Raphael, based on the novel by Arthur Schnitzler *Cinematography* Larry Smith *Set Decoration* Lisa Leone and Terry Wells *Original Music* Jocelyn Pook *Film Editing* Nigel Galt *Produced by* Stanley Kubrick. With Tom Cruise (Dr. William Harford), Nicole Kidman (Alice Harford), Sydney Pollack (Victor Ziegler), Todd Field (Nick Nightingale), Sky

du Mont (Sandor Szavost), Julienne Davis (Mandy), Vinessa Shaw (Domino), Rade Serbedzija (Milich), Leelee Sobieski (Milich's Daughter), Leon Vitali (Red Cloak), Alan Cumming (Desk Clerk), Fay Masterson (Sally).

Magnolia
Directed by Paul Thomas Anderson *Screenplay* Paul Thomas Anderson *Cinematography* Robert Elswit *Set Decoration* Chris L. Spellman *Original Music* Jon Brion *Film Editing* Dylan Tichenor *Produced by* Paul Thomas Anderson and JoAnne Sellar. With Julianne Moore (Linda Partridge), William H. Macy (Donnie Smith), John C. Reilly (Officer Jim Kurring), Tom Cruise (Frank T.J. Mackey), Philip Baker Hall (Jimmy Gator), Philip Seymour Hoffman (Phil Parma), Jason Robards (Earl Partridge), Alfred Molina (Solomon Solomon), Melora Walters (Claudia Wilson Gator), Michael Bowen (Rick Spector), Ricky Jay (Burt Ramsey), April Grace (Gwenovier), Luis Guzman (Luis), Henry Gibson (Thurston howell), Felicity Huffman (Cynthia), Pat Healy (Young Pharmacy Kid), Patton Oswalt (Delmer Darion), Thomas Jane (Young Jimmy Gator).

2000
Mission: Impossible II
Directed by John Woo *Screenplay* Robert Towne *Cinematography* Jeffrey L. Kimball *Set Decoration* Kerrie Brown and Lauri Gaffin *Original Music* Hans Zimmer *Film Editing* Steven Kemper and Christian Wagner *Produced by* Tom Cruise and Paula Wagner. With Tom Cruise (Ethan Hunt), Dougray Scott (Sean Ambrose), Thandi Newton (Nyah Nordoff-Hall), Ving Rhames (Luther Stickell), Richard Roxburgh (Hugh Stamp), John Polson (Billy Baird), Brendan Gleeson (John C. McCloy), Rade Serbedzija

(Dr. Nekhorvich), William Mapother (Wallis), Anthony Hopkins (Mission Commander Swanbeck).

2001
Vanilla Sky
Directed by Cameron Crowe *Screenplay* Cameron Crowe *Cinematography* John Toll *Set Decoration* Cloudia Rebar *Original Music* Nancy Wilson *Film Editing* Joe Hutshing and Mark Livolsi *Produced by* Cameron Crowe, Tom Cruise and Paula Wagner. With Tom Cruise (David Aames), Penelope Cruz (Sofia Serrano), Cameron Diaz (Julie Gianni), Kurt Russell (McCabe), Jason Lee (Brian Shelby), Noah Taylor (Edmund Ventura), Tomothy Spall (Thomas Tipp), Tilda Swinton (Rebecca Dearborn), Michael Shannon (Aaron), Delaina Mitchell (David's Assistant), Shalom Harlow (Colleen), Tommy Lee (Frozen Vintage Car Man), Steven Spielberg (Guest at David Aames' Party).

2002
Minority Report
Directed by Steven Spielberg *Screenplay* Scott Frank and Jon Cohen, based on the short story by Philip K. Dick *Cinematography* Janusz Kaminski *Set Decoration* Anne Kuljian *Original Music* John Williams *Film Editing* Michael Kahn *Produced by* Jan de Bont, Bonnie Curtis, Gerald R. Molen, Walter F. Parkes. With Tom Cruise (Chief John Anderton), Max von Sydow (Director Lamar Burgess), Steve Harris (Jad), Neal McDonough (Fletcher), Patrick Kilpatrick (Knott), Jessica Capshaw (Evanna), Jim Rash (Technician), Colin Farrell (Danny Witwer), Samantha Morton (Agatha), Tim Blake Nelson (Gideon), Jessica Harper (Anne Lively), Paul Thomas Anderson (Passenger on Train), Cameron Crowe (Bus Passenger), Cameron Diaz (Bus Passenger).

2003
The Last Samurai
Directed by Edward Zwick *Screenplay* John Logan, Edward Zwick, and Marshall Herskovitz *Cinematography* John Toll *Set Decoration* Gretchen Rau *Original Music* Hans Zimmer *Film Editing* Victor Du Bois and Steven Rosenblum *Produced by* Tom Cruise, Ted Field, Marshall Herskovitz, Scott Kroopf, Paula Wagner, and Edward Zwick. With Ken Watanabe (Katsumoto), Tom Cruise (Nathan Algren), Billy Connolly (Zebulon Gant), Tony Goldwyn (Colonel Bagley), Masato Harada (Omura), Masashi Odate (Omura's Companion), John Koyama (Omura's Bodyguard), Timothy Spall (Simon Graham), Shichinosuke Nakamura (Emperor Meiji), Togo Igawa (General Hasegawa), Shin Koyamada (Nobutada), Hiroyuki Sanada (Ujio), Koyuki (Taka).

2004
Collateral
Directed by Michael Mann *Screenplay* Stuart Beattie *Cinematography* Din Beebe and Paul Cameron *Set Decoration* Sandy Reynolds-Wasco *Original Music* James Newton Howard *Film Editing* Jim Miller and Paul Rubell *Produced by* Michael Mann and Julie Richardson. With Tom Cruise (Vincent), Jamie Foxx (Max), Jada Pinkett Smith (Annie), Mark Ruffalo (Fanning), Peter Berg (Richard Weidner), Bruce McGill (Pedrosa), Irma P. Hall (Ida), Barry Shabaka Henley (Daniel), Bodhi Elfman (Young Professional Man), Debi Mazar (Young Professional Woman), Javier Barden (Felix), Emilio Rivera (Paco), Jason Statham (Airport Man).

2005
War of the Worlds
Directed by Steven Spielberg *Screenplay* Josh Friedman and David Koepp, based on the

novel by H.G. Wells *Cinematography* Janusz Kaminski *Set Decoration* Anne Kuljian *Original Music* John Williams *Film Editing* Michael Kahn *Produced by* Kathleen Kennedy and Colin Wilson. With Tom Cruise (Ray Ferrier), Dakota Fanning (Rachel Ferrier), Miranda Otto (Mary Anne), Justin Chatwin (Robbie), Tim Robbins (Harlan Ogilvy), Rick Gonzalez (Vincent), Yul Vazquez (Julio), Lenny Venito (Manny the Mechanic), Lisa Ann Walter (Bartender), Ann Robinson (Grandmother), Gene Barry (Grandfather), David Alan Basche (Tim), Amy Ryan (Neighbor with Toddler).

2006
Mission: Impossible III
Directed by J.J. Abrams *Screenplay* Alex Kurtzman, Roberto Orci and J.J. Abram *Cinematography* Daniel Mindel *Set Decoration* Karen Manthey *Original Music* Michael Giacchino *Film Editing* Maryann Brandon and Mary Jo Markey *Produced by* Tom Cruise and Paula Wagner. With Tom Cruise (Ethan Hunt), Philip Seymour Hoffman (Owen Davian), Ving Rhames (Luther Stickell), Billy Crudup (John Musgrave), Michelle Monaghan (Julia), Jonathan Rhys Meyers (Declan Gormley), Keri Russell (Lindsey Farris), Maggie Q (Zhen Lei), Simon Pegg (Benji Dunn), Eddie Marsan (Brownway), Laurence Fishburne (Theodore Brassel), Aaron Paul (Rick).

2007
Lions for Lambs
Directed by Robert Redford *Screenplay* Matthew Michael Carnahan *Cinematography* Philippe Rousselot *Set Decoration* Leslie A. Pope *Original Music* Mark Isham *Film Editing* Joe Hutshing *Produced by* Matthew Michael Carnahan, Tracy Falco, Andrew Hauptman and

Robert Redford. With Robert Redford (Professor Stephen Malley), Meryl Streep (Janine Roth), Tom Cruise (Senator Jasper Irving), Michael Pena (Ernest Rodriguez), Andrew Garfield (Todd Hayes), Peter Berg (Lt. Col. Falco), Kevin Dunn (ANX Editor), Derek Luke (Arian Finch).

2008
Tropic Thunder
Directed by Ben Stiller *Screenplay* Justin Theroux, Ben Stiller, and Etan Cohen *Cinematography* John Toll *Set Decoration* Daniel B. Clancy *Original Music* Theodore Shapiro *Film Editing* Greg Hayden *Produced by* Stuart Cornfeld, Eric McLeod, and Ben Stiller. With Robert Downey Jr. (Kirk Lazarus), Jack Black (Jeff Portnoy), Jay Baruchel (Kevin Sandusky), Brandon T. Jackson (Alpa Chino), Ben Stiller (Tugg Speedman), Steve Coogan (Damien Cockburn), Danny McBride (Cody), Bill Hader (Studio Executive Rob Slolom), Nick Nolte (Four Leaf Tayback), Christine Taylor (Rebecca), Matthew McConaughey (Rick Peck), Yvette Nicole Brown (Peck's Assistant), Reggie Lee (Byong), Trieu Tran (Tru), Brandon Soohoo (Tran), Tom Cruise (Les Grossman), Tobey Maguire (Himself).

Valkyrie
Directed by Bryan Singer *Screenplay* Christopher McQuarrie and Nathan Alexander *Cinematography* Newton Thomas Sigel *Set Decoration* Bernhard Henrich *Original Music* John Ottman *Film Editing* John Ottman *Produced by* Gilbert Adler, Christopher McQuarrie and Bryan Singer. With Tom Cruise (Colonel Claus von Stauffenberg), Kenneth Branagh (Major-General Henning von Tresckow), Bill Nighy (General Friedrich Olbright), Tom Wilkinson (General Friedrich Fromm),

Carice van Houten (Nina von Stauffenberg), Thomas Kretschmann (Major Otto Ernst Remer), Terence Stamp (Ludwig Beck), Eddie Issard (General Erich Fellgiebel).

2010
Knight and Day
Directed by James Mangold *Screenplay* Patrick O'Neill *Cinematography* Phedon Papamichael *Set Decoration* Jay Hart *Original Music* John Powell *Film Editing* Quincy Z. Gunderson and Michael McCusker *Produced by* Todd Garner, Cathy Konrad and Steve Pink. With Tom Cruise (Roy Miller), Cameron Diaz (June Havens), Peter Sarsgaard (John Fitzgerald), Jordi Molla (Antonio Quintana), Viola Davis (Isabel George), Paul Dano (Simon Feck), Falk Hentschel (Bernhard), Marc Blucas (Rodney), Lennie Loftin (Braces), Maggie Grace (April Havens), Gal Gadot (Naomi).

2011
Mission: Impossible—Ghost Protocol
Directed by Brad Bird *Screenplay* Josh Appelbaum and Andrew Nemec *Cinematography* Robert Elswit *Set Decoration* Rosemary Brandenburg, Andronico Del Rosario, and Elizabeth Wilcox *Original Music* Michael Giacchino *Film Editing* Paul Hirsch *Produced by* J.J. Abrams, Bryan Burk and Tom Cruise. With Tom Cruise (Ethan Hunt), Paula Patton (Jane Carter), Simon Pegg (Benji Dunn), Jeremy Renner (William Brandt), Michael Nyqvist (Kurt Hendricks), Vladimir Mashkov (Anatoly Sidorov), Samuli Edelmann (Wistrom), Ivan Shvedoff (Leonid Lisenker), Anil Kapoor (Brij Nath), Lea Seydoux (Sabine Moreau), Josh Holloway (Trevor Hanaway), Michelle Monaghan (Julia Meade), Ving Rhames (Luther Stickell), Tom Wilkinson (IMF Secretary).

2012
Rock of Ages
Directed by Adam Shankman *Screenplay* Justin Theroux, Chris D'Arienzo, Allan Loeb *Cinematography* Bojan Bazelli *Set Decoration* Xavier Cortes and K.C. Fox *Original Music* Adam Anders and Peer Astrom *Film Editing* Emma E. Hickox *Produced by* Jennifer Gibgot, Garrett Grant, Carl Levin, Tobey Maguire, Scott Prisand, and Matt Weaver. With Julianne Hough (Sherrie Christian), Diego Boneta (Drew Boley), Russell Brand (Lonny), Alec Baldwin (Dennis Dupree), Bryan Cranston (Mike Whitmore), Catherine Zeta-Jones (Patricia Whitmore), Paul Giamatti (Paul Gill), Tom Cruise (Stacee Jaxx), Malin Akerman (Constance Sack), Will Forte (Mitch Miley), Mary J. Blige (Justice), Eli Roth (Stefano), Nuno Bettencourt (Rocker), Deborah Gibson (Rocker), Sebastian Bach (Rocker).

Jack Reacher
Directed by Christopher McQuarrie *Screenplay* Christopher McQuarrie, based on the novel by Lee Child *Cinematography* Caleb Deschanel *Set Decoration* Douglas A. Mowat *Original Music* Joe Kramer *Film Editing* Kevin Stitt *Produced by* Tom Cruise, Don Granger, Gary Levinsohn, and Paula Wagner. With Tom Cruise (Jack Reacher), Rosamund Pike (Helen), Richard Jenkins (Rodin), David Oyelowo (Emerson), Wener Herzog (The Zec), Jai Courtney (Charlie), Vladimir Sizov (Vlad), Joseph Sikora (Barr), Michael Raymond-James (Linsky), Alexia Fast (Sandy), Josh Helman (Jeb), Robert Duvall (Cash), Lee Child (Desk Sergeant).

2013
Oblivion
Directed by Joseph Kosinski *Screenplay* Karl Gajdusek and Michael Arndt, based on the

graphic novel by Joseph Kosinski *Cinematography* Claudio Miranda *Set Decoration* Ronald R. Reiss *Original Music* Anthony Gonzalez, M.8.3., Joseph Trapanese *Film Editing* Richard Francis-Bruce *Produced by* Peter Chernin, Dylan Clark, Duncan Henderson, Joseph Kosinski, and Barry Levine. With Tom Cruise (Jack), Morgan Freeman (Beech), Olga Kurylenko (Julia), Andrea Riseborough (Victoria), Nikolaj Coster-Waldau (Sykes), Melissa Leo (Sally), Zoe Bell (Kara), Abigail Lowe.

Edge of Tomorrow
Directed by Doug Liman *Screenplay* Dante Harper, Joby Harper, Alex Kurtzman, Christopher McQuarrie, and Roberto Orci, based on the novel by Hiroshi Sakurazaka *Cinematography* Dion Beebe *Set Decoration* Elli Griff *Original Music* Daniel Rutter *Film Editing* James Herbert *Produced by* Jason Hoffs, Gregory Jacobs, Tom Lassally, Jeffrey Silver, and Erwin Stoff. With Tom Cruise (Lt. Col. Bill Cage), Emily Cage (Rita Vrataski), Bill Paxton (TBD), Jeremy Piven (Col. Walter Marx), Lara Pulver (Karen Lord), Marianne Jean-Baptiste (Dr. Whittle), Tony Way (Kimmel).

Cruise in Steven Spielberg's *Minority Report* (2002).

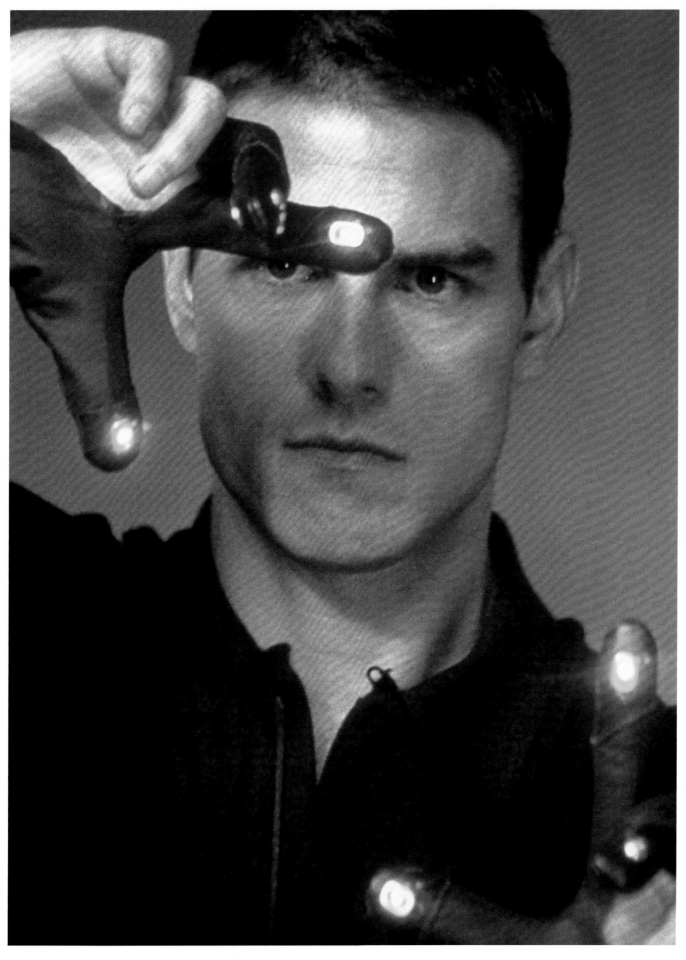

Articles

Rachel Abramowitz, "Scared Silly," *L.A. Times*, May 8, 2005.

David Ansen, "Cruise Guns for the Top," *Newsweek*, July 9, 1986.

George Anthony, "Hunk Sits at the Feet of Old Pro," *Toronto Sun*, December 9, 1988.

Paul Attanasio, "*Top Gun*: Where the Flyboys Are," *The Washington Post*, May 19, 1986.

Paul Attanasio, "The Twin Titans of *Top Gun*," *The Washington Post*, May 16, 1986.

Jonathan Benair, "*Top Gun*," *Los Angeles Style*, April 1987.

Geoff Boucher, "*Mission: Impossible*: Brad Bird Goes into Cruise Control," *L.A. Times*, November 2, 2011.

Geoff Boucher, "Tom Cruise Has Fervent Fan in *Mission: Impossible* Director," *L.A. Times*, September 29, 2011.

Liz Braun, "Tom Cruise, Katie Holmes to Divorce," *Toronto Sun*, June 29, 2012.

Pat H. Broeske, "Cruise-ing in the Media Stratosphere," *L.A. Times Calendar*, May 25, 1986.

Anita M. Bush, "Rice Takes on Kingsley in Latest *Vampire* Round," *Hollywood Reporter*, May 4, 1994.

Jess Cagle, "About Tom," *Time*, June 24, 2002.

Vincent Canby, "Vintage Plotting Propels Mach II Planes in *Top Gun*,"

The New York Times, June 8, 1986.

"Chatter," *People*, April 17, 1989.

Kim Christensen and Claire Hoffman, "Viacom to Break Ties with Cruise," *L.A. Times*, August 23, 2006.

George Christy, "The Great Life," *Hollywood Reporter*, September 24, 1996.

Michael Cieply, "Tom Cruise, in Bit Role, Nips Studio's Top Gun," *The New York Times*, April 3, 2008.

"Clips," *Hollywood Reporter*, October 20, 1994.

Nancy Collins, "Tom Cruise," *Us*, June 30, 1986.

Jennet Conant, "Lestat, C'est Moi," *Esquire*, March 1994.

Christopher Connelly, "Top Gun Tom Cruise," *Rolling Stone*, June 19, 1986.

Richard Corliss, "Tom Terrific," *Time*, December 25, 1989.

Dan Cox, "Zellweger to Limn Love of Jerry Maguire's Life," *Variety*, January 24, 1996.

Cameron Crowe, "Conversations with Cruise," *Vanity Fair*, June 2000.

Cameron Crowe, "Hot Shot in *Top Gun*," *Interview*, May 1986.

Cameron Crowe, "The Jerry Maguire Journal," *Rolling Stone*, December 26, 1996.

"Cries and Whispers," *Hollywood Reporter*, July 6, 1999.

"Cries and Whispers," *Hollywood Reporter*, December 28, 1999.

"Cruise, Kidman Win Apology, Settlement," *South Florida Sun-Sentinel*, October 30, 1998.

"Cruise Raises Funds for 9/11 Workers," *The Washington Post*, April 20, 2007.

Manohla Dargis, "Falling Off Skyscrapers Sometimes Hurts a Bit," *The New York Times*, Dec. 15, 2011.

Daina Darzin, "Cruisin'," *Ampersand*, Fall 1986.

David Denby, "Days of Rage," *New York*, December 18, 1989.

David Denby, "Good Sports," *New York*, December 16, 1996.

David Denby, "Pop Gun," *New York*, May 19, 1986.

David Denby, "Supply-side Hero," *New York*, August 22, 1983.

Bill Desowitz, "Kubrick's Depth of Field," *L.A. Times*, July 30, 1999.

Elaine Dutka, "Interview with the Vampire's Picky Creator," *L.A. Times*, August 22, 1993.

Elaine Dutka, "The Latest Exorcism of Oliver Stone," *L.A. Times*, Dec. 17, 1989.

Roger Ebert, "Risky Business," *Chicago Sun-Times*, August 17, 1983.

David Eimer, "Talking Ballpark Figures with *Jerry Maguire* Director Cameron Crowe," *Neon*, April 1997.

Claudia Eller, "Day-Lewis' Agent Sinks Stake in *Vampire* Claim," *Variety*, February 16, 1993.

Steve Erickson, "Stunted," *LA Weekly*, July 2, 1993.

"Fainting Spells Reported During July Screenings," *Variety*, January 11, 1990.

"Fang-fare," *Variety*, August 2, 1993.

Michael Fleming, "Tom Cruise," *Playboy*, June 2012.

Cal Fussman, "Tom Cruise: The Fixer," *Esquire*, June 7, 2010.

Trip Gabriel, "Cruise at the Crossroads," *Rolling Stone*, January 11, 1990.

Lou Gaul, "Cruise Control," *Home Viewer*, November 1986.

Jeff Giles, "Walk on the Wild Side," *Newsweek*, December 20, 1999.

Merle Ginsberg, "Major Tom," *W*, January 1997.

Merle Ginsberg, "Paul Thomas Anderson: W Pioneers Filmmaker," *W*, November 1999.

Greg Gittrich, "Bravest Taking Cruise Cure," *NY Daily News*, Dec. 13, 2003.

Walter Goodman, "The Screen: *Top Gun*, a Tale of Navy Airmen," *The New York Times*, May 16, 1986.

Betty Goodwin, "Fame Came Fast for Actor Tom Cruise," *Los Angeles Herald-Examiner*, Oct. 22, 1983.

Lee Grant, "Summer's Hottest Faces," *L.A. Times*, August 31, 1983.

James Greenberg, "*Top Gun*," *Variety*, May 9, 1986.

Ray Greene, "Man with a Mission," *Boxoffice*, April 1996.

John Harlow, "Alien Epic Launches Cruise into £200 Stellar League," *Sunday Times* (London), September 5, 2004.

Ellen Hawkes, "I Had to Grow Up So Fast," *Parade*, January 8, 1989.

Courtney Hazlett, "Tom Cruise's Fat-Suit Fracas," MSNBC.com, November 19, 2007.

Bill Higgins, "Creatures of the Night," *L.A. Times*, November 11, 1994.

Bill Higgins, "*Rock of Ages'* Tom Cruise Proved He Could Lip-Sync in 1983," *Hollywood Reporter*, June 22, 2012.

Hal Hinson, "Fear and Desire," *New Times LA*, July 15, 1999.

Lynn Hirschberg, "A Conversation with Tom Cruise," *Rolling Stone*, August 11, 1988.

Lynn Hirschberg, "His Way," *The New York Times Magazine*, Dec. 19, 1999.

J. Hoberman, "Phallus in Wonderland," *Village Voice*, May 27, 1986.

Steve Hochman, "Fast Times, Indeed," *L.A. Times*, December 26, 1996.

David Hutchings, "In the Risky Business of Box Office and Breaking Hearts, Tom Cruise Is a Top Gun," *People*, June 21, 1986.

David Hutchings, "No Wonder Tom Cruise Is Sitting Pretty—*Risky Business* Has Paid Off in Stardom," *People*, September 5, 1983.

Dave Itzkoff, "Spoof Within a Movie Within a Movie Within..." *The New York Times*, August 10, 2008.

Pauline Kael, "Brutes," *The New Yorker*, June 16, 1986.

Pauline Kael, "Sex and Politics," *The New Yorker*, September 5, 1983.

Larry Kart, "Movie Legend Michael Powell Tells How He Worked His Cinematic Magic," *Chicago Tribune*, March 23, 1986.

Stanley Kauffmann, "Flash and Fraud," *New Republic*, September 19, 1983.

Bruce Kirkland, "Rebels with Random Causes," *Marquee*, March/April 1994.

Nancy Kolomitz, "*Top Gun*," *Film Journal*, June 1986.

Jesse Kornbluth, "Cruise Control," *Vanity Fair*, January 1989.

David Kronske, "He Accepted the Mission," *L.A. Times*, May 12, 1996.

Charla Krupp, "*Top Gun*: The Selling of Tom Cruise," *Glamour*, July 1986.

Chris Lee, "Looking for Action, He Got It," *L.A. Times*, August 10, 2008.

Rod Lurie, "No More Mr. Nice Guy," *Los Angeles Magazine*, October 1993.

"Mail," *People*, May 30, 1994.

Stephanie Mansfield, "Tom Cruise from the Neck Up," *GQ*, December 1992.

Merissa Marr, "Sumner Redstone Gives Tom Cruise His Walking Papers," *The Wall Street Journal*, August 23, 2006.

Andy Marx, "Cruise Bites on *Vampire*," *Variety*, July 26, 1993.

Pamela McClintock, "Tropical Punch," *Variety*, August 18, 2008.

Mia McNiece, "25 Years Ago! *Top Gun*," *People*, June 20, 2011.

Michael Mills, "Tom Cruise: Back in Action," *Moviegoer*, Dec. 1985.

"Mogul on a Mission," *Variety*, May 7, 2008.

Chris Mundy, "Slipping Around the Road with Brad Pitt," *Rolling Stone*, December 1, 1994.

Michael Musto, "NY Mirror," *Village Voice*, Feb. 1, 2000.

Tom O'Neill, "Tom Cruise Has It Covered," *Us*, January, 1993.

"People," *Time*, Aug. 12, 1985.

Charles P. Pierce, "The Player," *GQ*, December 1996.

Nick Pinkerton, "Man on a Mission," *Village Voice*, December 14, 2011.

Jonathan Powers, "*Top Gun*," *LA Weekly*, May 16, 1986.

Dotson Rader, "Who's to Say What's Normal?" *Parade*, April 9, 2006.

Frederic Raphael, "A Kubrick Odyssey," *The New Yorker*, June 14, 1999.

David Rensin, "20 Questions: Tom Cruise," *Playboy*, July 1986.

David Rensin, "Straight Talk," *Us*, January 22, 1990.

Anne Rice, "A Special Message from Anne Rice to Her Readers," *Variety*, December 23, 1994.

"*Risky Business*," *Village Voice*, August 16, 1983.

Dan Sallitt, "Brickman Chances It in *Risky Business*," *Reader*, August 12, 1983.

Mark Sanderson, "Cruise Control," *Time Out*, March 1, 1987.

Robert Scheer, "The Playboy Interview: Tom Cruise," *Playboy*, January 1990.

Richard Schickel, "All Eyes on Them," *Time*, July 5, 1999.

Peter Sciretta, "Interview: Todd Field Part 2," Slashfilm.com, October 26, 2006.

Walter Scott, "Walter Scott's Personality Parade," *Parade*, May 15, 2005.

Kevin Sessums, "Cruise Speed," *Vanity Fair*, October 1994.

Richard Setlowe, "A Reluctant Pilot, Scott Soared to Top with *Gun*," *Variety*, August 6, 1996.

Ingrid Sischy, "The Interview, the Vampire, the Actor," *Interview*, November 1994.

Gene Siskel, "For Tom Cruise, Movie Career No Longer Risky Business," *Santa Monica Evening Outlook*, July 29, 1988.

Liz Smith, "Those Bloody Rumors," *L.A. Times*, August 28, 1993.

Liz Smith, "Tom Cruise's Grossest Deal," *L.A. Times*, July 15, 1993.

Liz Smith, "Tom Has Taste for Bad-Guy Role," *L.A. Times*, July 19, 1993.

Sean Smith, "Fear Factor," *Newsweek*, June 27, 2005.

Sean Smith, "The King of the Worlds," *Newsweek*, June 27, 2006.

"Spy," *Hello!* October 18, 2010

Chuck Stephens, "Paul Thomas Anderson Lets It All Hang Out," *Village Voice*, December 21, 1999.

Joe Stevens, "Outrageous Example," *Long Beach Press-Telegram*, March 20, 2000.

Bob Strauss, "The Time of Her Life," *Long Beach Press-Telegram*, July 21, 1999.

Jimmy Summers, "*Top Gun*," *Ampersand*, Summer 1986.

Benjamin Svetkey, "Eyes of the Storm," *Entertainment Weekly*, July 23, 1999.

David Thomson, "*Magnolia*," *The Independent*, February 20, 2000.

"Tom Cruise Opens Up About His Beliefs in the Church of Scientology," *Der Spiegel*, April 27, 2005.

"Tom Cruise Stands Firm on 9/11 Medication Comments at Gala," Hollywood.com, December 16, 2005.

Christopher Tricarico, "Top Dollar," *L.A. Times*, June 8, 1986.

Mim Udovitch, "The Epic Obsessions of Paul Thomas Anderson," *Rolling Stone*, February 3, 2000.

Bernard Weintraub, "*Boogie* Writer Back in Valley," *The New York Times*, October 8, 1999.

Robert W. Welkos, "Ears Wide Open for News of Kubrick's Latest," *L.A. Times*, May 13, 1997.

Books

Lester D. Friedman, *Citizen Spielberg*, Champaign: University of Illinois Press, 2006.

Charles Fleming, *High Concept: Don Simpson and the Hollywood Culture of Excess.* New York: Main Street Books, 1999.

Rob Lowe, *Stories I Only Tell My Friends*, New York: Henry Holt and Co., 2011.

1 Robert Scheer, "The Playboy Interview: Tom Cruise," *Playboy*, January 1990.

2 Bruce Kirkland, "Rebels with Random Causes," *Marquee*, March/April 1994.

3 Robert Scheer, *op. cit.*

4 Daina Darzin, "Cruisin'," *Ampersand*, Fall 1986.

5 Robert Scheer, *op. cit.*

6 Ellen Hawkes, "I Had to Grow Up So Fast," *Parade*, January 8, 1989.

7 *Ibid.*

8 Dotson Rader, "Who's to Say What's Normal?" *Parade*, April 9, 2006.

9 Lynn Hirschberg, "A Conversation with Tom Cruise," *Rolling Stone*, August 11, 1988.

10 Christopher Connelly, "Top Gun Tom Cruise," *Rolling Stone*, June 19, 1986.

11 *Ibid.*

12 Lynn Hirschberg, *op. cit.*

13 Stephanie Mansfield, "Tom Cruise from the Neck Up," *GQ*, December 1992.

14 Christopher Connelly, *op. cit.*

15 Tom O'Neill, "Tom Cruise Has It Covered," *Us*, January 1993.

16 *Taps* press notes, 1981.

17 Robert Scheer, *op. cit.*

18 Michael Mills, "Tom Cruise: Back in Action," *Moviegoer*, December 1985.

19 Mim Udovitch, "The Epic Obsessions of Paul Thomas Anderson," *Rolling Stone*, February 3, 2000.

20 Bernard Weintraub, "*Boogie* Writer Back in Valley," *The New York Times*, October 8, 1999.

21 Robert Scheer, *op. cit.*

22 Dotson Rader, *op. cit.*

23 David Ansen "Cruise Guns for the Top," *Newsweek*, July 9, 1986.

24 Lynn Hirschberg, *op. cit.*

25 David Rensin, "20 Questions: Tom Cruise," *Playboy*, July 1986.

26 Trip Gabriel, "Cruise at the Crossroads," *Rolling Stone*, January 11, 1990.

27 Dan Sallitt, "Brickman Chances It in *Risky Business*," *Reader*, August 12, 1983.

28 Christopher Connelly, *op. cit.*

29 Michael Mills, *op. cit.*

30 Cameron Crowe, "Hot Shot in *Top Gun*," *Interview*, May 1986.

31 Rob Lowe, *Stories I Only Tell My Friends*, Henry Holt and Co., 2011, p. 101.

32 Cameron Crowe, "Conversations with Cruise," *Vanity Fair*, June 2000.

33 Cameron Crowe, "Hot Shot," *op cit.*.

34 *Risky Business: 25th Anniversary Edition*, commentary track, DVD, 2008.

35 Cameron Crowe, "Hot Shot," *op. cit.*

36 Bill Higgins, "*Rock of Ages*' Tom Cruise Proved He Could Lip-Sync in 1983," *Hollywood Reporter*, June 22, 2012.

37 Cameron Crowe, "Conversations," *op. cit.*

38 David Hutchings, "No Wonder Tom Cruise Is Sitting Pretty—*Risky Business* Has Paid Off in Stardom," *People*, September 5, 1983.

39 Betty Goodwin, "Fame Came Fast for Actor Tom Cruise," *Los Angeles Herald-Examiner*, October 22, 1983.

40 *Risky Business: 25th Anniversary Edition*, *op. cit.*

41 Christopher Connelly, *op. cit.*

42 *Risky Business: 25th Anniversary Edition*, *op. cit.*

43 Nancy Collins, "Tom Cruise," *Us*, June 30, 1986.

44 *Risky Business: 25th Anniversary Edition*, *op. cit.*

45 *Ibid.*

46 *Ibid.*

47 *Ibid.*

48 Gene Siskel, "For Tom Cruise, Movie Career No Longer Risky Business," *Santa Monica Evening Outlook*, July 29, 1988.

49 David Rensin, *op. cit.*

50 Roger Ebert, "Risky Business," *Chicago Sun-Times*, August 17, 1983.

51 "Risky Business," *Village Voice*, August 16, 1983.

52 Pauline Kael, "Sex and Politics," *The New Yorker*, September 5, 1983.

53 Stanley Kauffmann, "Flash and Fraud," *New Republic*, September 19, 1983.

54 David Denby, "Supply-side Hero," *New York*, August 22, 1983.

55 Lee Grant, "Summer's Hottest Faces," *Los Angeles Times*, August 31, 1983.

56 Pat H. Broeske, "Cruise-ing in the Media Stratosphere," *Los Angeles Times*, May 25, 1986.

57 David Hutchings, *op. cit.*

58 Lee Grant, *op. cit.*

59 Lynn Hirschberg,, *op. cit.*

60 Larry Kart, "Movie Legend Michael Powell Tells How He Worked His Cinematic Magic," *Chicago Tribune*, March 23, 1986.

61 Paul Attanasio, "The Twin Titans of *Top Gun*," *The Washington Post*, May 16, 1986.

62 *Top Gun* press notes, 1986.

63 *Top Gun*, Widescreen Special Collector's Edition, 2004.

64 Richard Setlowe, "A Reluctant Pilot, Scott Soared to Top with *Gun*," *Variety*, August 6, 1996.

65 Charles Fleming, *High Concept: Don Simpson and the Hollywood Culture of Excess*, Main Street Books, 1999, p. 71.

66 Lynn Hirschberg, *op. cit.*

67 Cameron Crowe, "Conversations," *op. cit.*

68 Christopher Connelly, *op. cit.*

69 Jesse Kornbluth, "Cruise Control," *Vanity Fair*, January 1989.

70 David Rensin, *op. cit.*

71 Lou Gaul, "Cruise Control," *Home Viewer*, November 1986.

72 Stephanie Mansfield, *op. cit.*

73 David Hutchings, "In the Risky Business of Box Office and Breaking Hearts, Tom Cruise Is a Top Gun," *People*, June 21, 1986.

74 Charles Fleming, *op. cit.*

75 *Ibid.*

76 Mia McNiece, "25 Years Ago! *Top Gun*," *People*, June 20, 2011.

77 David Ansen, *op. cit.*

78 *Top Gun* DVD, *op. cit.*

79 Jimmy Summers, "*Top Gun*," *Ampersand*, Summer 1986.

80 David Ansen, *op. cit.*

81 *Top Gun* DVD, *op. cit.*

82 *Ibid.*

83 Jonathan Benair, "*Top Gun*," *L.A. Style*, April 1987.

84 Vincent Canby, "Vintage Plotting Propels Mach II Planes in *Top Gun*," *The New York Times*, June 8, 1986.

85 Jonathan Powers, "*Top Gun*," *LA Weekly*, May 16, 1986.

86 "People," *Time*, August 12, 1985.

87 J. Hoberman, "Phallus in Wonderland," *Village Voice*, May 27, 1986.

88 Nancy Kolomitz, "*Top Gun*," *Film Journal*, June 1986.

89 David Denby, "Pop Gun," *New York*, May 19, 1986.

90 Paul Attanasio, "*Top Gun*: Where the Flyboys Are," *The Washington Post*, May 19, 1986.

91 Walter Goodman, "The Screen: *Top Gun*, a Tale of Navy Airmen," *The New York Times*, May 16, 1986.

92 Christopher Tricarico, "Top Dollar," *Los Angeles Times*, June 8, 1986.

93 Charla Krupp, "*Top Gun*: The Selling of Tom Cruise," *Glamour*, July 1986.

94 Christopher Connelly, *op. cit.*

95 *Top Gun* DVD, *op. cit.*

96 Pauline Kael, "Brutes," *The New Yorker*, June 16, 1986.

97 James Greenberg, "*Top Gun*," *Variety*, May 9, 1986.

98 George Anthony, "Hunk Sits at the Feet of Old Pro," *Toronto Sun*, December 9, 1988.

99 Cameron Crowe, "Conversations," *op. cit.*

100 *Ibid.*

101 Richard Corliss, "Tom Terrific," *Time*, December 25, 1989.

102 Robert Scheer, *op. cit.*

103 George Anthony, *op. cit.*

104 Trip Gabriel, *op. cit.*

105 Gene Siskel, *op. cit.*

106 Trip Gabriel, *op. cit.*

107 Gene Siskel *op. cit.*

108 *Ibid.*

109 "Chatter," *People*, April 17, 1989.

110 Elaine Dutka, "The Latest Exorcism of Oliver Stone," *Los Angeles Times*, December 17, 1989.

111 Richard Corliss, *op. cit.*

112 *Ibid.*

113 Elaine Dutka, *op. cit.*

114 David Rensin, "Straight Talk," *Us*, January 22, 1990.

115 Trip Gabriel, *op. cit.*

116 Elaine Dutka, *op. cit.*

117 Mark Sanderson, "Cruise Control," *Time Out*, March 1, 1987.

118 Richard Corliss, *op. cit.*

119 Elaine Dutka, *op. cit.*

120 Jesse Kornbluth, *op. cit.*

121 Richard Corliss, *op. cit.*

122 Elaine Dutka, *op. cit.*

123 "Fainting Spells Reported During July Screenings," *Variety*, January 11, 1990.

124 Robert Scheer, *op. cit.*

125 Elaine Dutka, *op. cit.*

126 *Ibid.*

127 Robert Scheer, *op. cit.*

128 Elaine Dutka, *op. cit.*

129 Robert Scheer, *op. cit.*

130 David Rensin, *op. cit.*

131 Richard Corliss, *op. cit.*

132 Robert Scheer, *op. cit.*

133 David Denby, "Days of Rage," *New York*, December 18, 1989.

134 Elaine Dutka, *op. cit.*

135 *Ibid.*

136 Claudia Eller, "Day-Lewis' Agent Sinks Stake in *Vampire* Claim," *Variety*, February 16, 1993.

137 Liz Smith, "Tom Cruise's Grossest Deal," *Los Angeles Times*, July 15, 1993.

138 Liz Smith, "Tom Has Taste for Bad-Guy Role," *Los Angeles Times*, July 19, 1993.

139 Andy Marx, "Cruise Bites on *Vampire*," *Variety*, July 26, 1993.

140 Steve Erickson, "Stunted," *LA Weekly*, July 2, 1993.

141 tephanie Mansfield, *op. cit.*

142 "Fang-fare," *Variety*, August 2, 1993.

143 *Interview with the Vampire*, Special Edition DVD, commentary track, 2000.

144 Elaine Dutka, "Interview with the Vampire's Picky Creator," *Los Angeles Times*, August 22, 1993.

145 Rod Lurie, "No More Mr. Nice Guy," *Los Angeles Magazine*, October 1993.

146 Jennet Conant, "Lestat, C'est Moi," *Esquire*, March 1994.

147 *Ibid.*

148 Ingrid Sischy, "The Interview, the Vampire, the Actor," *Interview*, November 1994.

149 Jennet Conant, *op. cit.*

150 Kevin Sessums, "Cruise Speed," *Vanity Fair*, October 1994.

151 *Ibid.*

152 "Mail," *People*, May 30, 1994.

153 Anita M. Bush, "Rice Takes on Kingsley in Latest *Vampire* Round," *Hollywood Reporter*, May 4, 1994.

154 Elaine Dutka, "Interview," *op. cit.*

155 Ingrid Sischy, *op. cit.*

156 Kevin Sessums, *op. cit.*

157 Chris Mundy, "Slipping Around the Road with Brad Pitt," *Rolling Stone*, December 1, 1994.

158 Liz Smith, "Those Bloody Rumors," *Los Angeles Times*, August 28, 1993.

159 Jennet Conant, *op. cit.*

160 Kevin Sessums, *op. cit.*

161 *Interview with the Vampire* DVD, commentary track, *op. cit.*

162 Kevin Sessums, *op. cit.*

163 Chris Mundy, *op. cit.*

164 Ingrid Sischy, *op. cit.*

165 *Ibid.*

166 Jennet Conant, *op. cit.*

167 Kevin Sessums, *op. cit.*

168 Ingrid Sischy, *op. cit.*

169 Anne Rice, "A Special Message from Anne Rice to Her Readers," *Variety*, December 23, 1994.

170 *Interview with the Vampire*, Special Edition DVD, Special Features, 2000.

171 Bill Higgins, "Creatures of the Night," *Los Angeles Times*, November 11, 1994.

172 Jennet Conant, *op. cit.*

173 Ingrid Sischy, *op. cit.*

174 *Interview with the Vampire* DVD, commentary track, *op. cit.*

175 Anne Rice, *op. cit.*

176 "Clips," *Hollywood Reporter*, October 20, 1994.

177 Anne Rice, *op. cit.*

178 Cameron Crowe, "Hot Shot," *op. cit.*

179 Cameron Crowe, "The Jerry Maguire Journal," *Rolling Stone*, December 26, 1996.

180 Cameron Crowe, "Hot Shot," *op. cit.*

181 Merle Ginsberg, "Major Tom," *W*, January 1997.

182 Cameron Crowe, "Maguire Journal," *op. cit.*

183 Merle Ginsberg, *op. cit.*

184 Cameron Crowe, "Maguire Journal," *op. cit.*

185 *Ibid.*

186 *Ibid.*

187 Dan Cox, "Zellweger to Limn Love of Jerry Maguire's Life," *Variety*, January 24, 1996.

188 David Eimer, "Talking Ballpark Figures with *Jerry Maguire* Director Cameron Crowe," *Neon*, April 1997.

189 Cameron Crowe, "Maguire Journal," *op. cit.*

190 Merle Ginsberg, *op. cit.*

191 Cameron Crowe, "Maguire Journal," *op. cit.*

192 *Jerry Maguire* production notes, 1996.

193 *Jerry Maguire*, Special Edition DVD, 1996.

194 Cameron Crowe, "Maguire Journal," *op. cit.*

195 Merle Ginsberg, *op. cit.*

196 Charles P. Pierce, "The Player," *GQ*, December 1996.

197 Cameron Crowe, "Maguire Journal," *op. cit.*

198 Steve Hochman, "Fast Times, Indeed," *Los Angeles Times*, December 26, 1996.

199 Jerry Maguire DVD, *op. cit.*

200 Merle Ginsberg, *op. cit.*

201 Cameron Crowe, "Maguire Journal," *op. cit.*

202 Merle Ginsberg, *op. cit.*

203 *Ibid.*

204 *Jerry Maguire* DVD, *op. cit.*

205 David Denby, "Good Sports," *New York*, December 16, 1996.

206 "Access Archives: Tom Cruise," *Access Hollywood*, http://watch.accesshollywood.com/video/access-archives:-tom-cruise/1309461879001.

207 David Kronske, "He Accepted the Mission,"

Los Angeles Times, May 12, 1996.

208 *Eyes Wide Shut*, Two-Disc Special Edition DVD, commentary track, 2008.

209 Frederic Raphael, "A Kubrick Odyssey," *The New Yorker*, June 14, 1999.

210 *Ibid.*

211 "Cries and Whispers," *Hollywood Reporter*, July 6, 1999.

212 *Eyes Wide Shut* DVD, *op. cit.*

213 *Ibid.*

214 Richard Schickel, "All Eyes on Them," *Time*, July 5, 1999.

215 Benjamin Svetkey, "Eyes of the Storm," *Entertainment Weekly*, July 23, 1999.

216 Lynn Hirschberg, *op. cit.*

217 Bob Strauss, "The Time of Her Life," *Long Beach Press-Telegram*, July 21, 1999.

218 *Eyes Wide Shut* DVD, op. cit.

219 Richard Schickel, *op. cit.*

220 Benjamin Svetkey, *op. cit.*

221 Robert W. Welkos, "Ears Wide Open for News of Kubrick's Latest," *Los Angeles Times*, May 13, 1997.

222 Peter Sciretta, "Interview: Todd Field Part 2," Slashfilm.com, October 26, 2006.

223 Hal Hinson, "Fear and Desire," *New Times LA*, July 15, 1999.

224 Bill Desowitz, "Kubrick's Depth of Field," *Los Angeles Times*, July 30, 1999.

225 Cameron Crowe, "Conversations," *op. cit.*

226 Richard Schickel, *op. cit.*

227 Mim Udovitch, *op. cit.*

228 Stephanie Mansfield, *op. cit.*

229 *Ibid.*

230 Christopher Connelly, "How Tom Cruise Keeps His Edge," *Talk*, April 2000.

231 Lynn Hirschberg, "His Way," *The New York*

Times Magazine, December 19, 1999.

232 "Cries and Whispers," *Hollywood Reporter*, December 28, 1999.

233 Merle Ginsberg, "Paul Thomas Anderson: W Pioneers Filmmaker" W, November 1999.

234 Jeff Giles, "Walk on the Wild Side," *Newsweek*, December 20, 1999.

235 Mim Udovitch, *op. cit.*

236 Michael Musto, "NY Mirror," *Village Voice*, February 1, 2000.

237 Jeff Giles, *op. cit.*

238 Chuck Stephens, "Paul Thomas Anderson Lets It All Hang Out," *Village Voice*, December 21, 1999.

239 Lynn Hirschberg, "His Way," *op. cit.*

240 Christopher Connelly, "His Edge," *op. cit.*

241 Joe Stevens, "Outrageous Example," *Long Beach Press-Telegram*, March 20, 2000.

242 *Ibid.*

243 Mim Udovitch, *op. cit.*

244 Cameron Crowe, "Conversations," *op. cit.*

245 *Ibid.*

246 *Ibid.*

247 Stephanie Mansfield, *op. cit.*

248 Sean Smith, "The King of the Worlds," *Newsweek*, June 27, 2006.

249 Jess Cagle, "About Tom," *Time*, June 24, 2002.

250 "Unscripted with Steven Spielberg and Tom Cruise," Moviefone, http://www.youtube.com/watch?v=LLxvFakk3tg.

251 Rachel Abramowitz, "Scared Silly," *Los Angeles Times*, May 8, 2005.

252 *Ibid.*

253 John Harlow, "Alien Epic Launches Cruise into £200 Stellar League," *The Sunday Times* (London), September 5, 2004.

254 Rachel Abramowitz, *op. cit.*

255 *Ibid.*

256 Walter Scott, "Walter Scott's Personality Parade," *Parade*, May 15, 2005.

257 Lester D. Friedman, *Citizen Spielberg*, University of Illinois Press, 2006, p. 156.

258 Rachel Abramowitz, *op. cit.*

259 *Ibid.*

260 *Ibid.*

261 The 74th Academy Awards, March 24, 2002.

262 Greg Gittrich, "Bravest Taking Cruise Cure," *New York Daily News*, December 13, 2003.

263 World Entertainment News Network, "Tom Cruise Stands Firm on 9/11 Medication Comments at Gala," Hollywood.com, December 16, 2005.

264 "Cruise Raises Funds for 9/11 Workers," *The Washington Post*, April 20, 2007.

265 Greg Gittrich, *op. cit.*

266 Rachel Abramowitz, *op. cit.*

267 Moviefone, *op. cit.*

268 David Rensin, *op.cit.*

269 "Cruise, Kidman Win Apology, Settlement," *South Florida Sun-Sentinel*, October 30, 1998.

270 Liz Braun, "Tom Cruise, Katie Holmes to Divorce," *Toronto Sun*, June 29, 2012.

271 *The Oprah Winfrey Show*, "Loving Life," May 23, 2005.

272 *Access Hollywood*, May 26, 2005.

273 *The Today Show*, June 25, 2005.

274 *The Oprah Winfrey Show*, *op. cit.*

275 Merissa Marr, "Sumner Redstone Gives Tom Cruise His Walking Papers," *The Wall Street Journal*, August 23, 2006.

276 Kim Christensen and Claire Hoffman, "Viacom to Break Ties with Cruise," *Los Angeles Times*, August 23, 2006.

277 Chris Lee, "Looking for Action, He Got It," *Los Angeles Times*, August 10, 2008.

278 Dave Itzkoff, "Spoof Within a Movie Within a Movie Within…" *The New York Times*, August 10, 2008.

279 Michael Cieply, "Tom Cruise, in Bit Role, Nips Studio's Top Gun," *The New York Times*, April 3, 2008.

280 Chris Lee, *op. cit.*

281 Dave Itzkoff, *op. cit.*

282 *Tropic Thunder* DVD, 2008.

283 *Ibid.*

284 Courtney Hazlett, "Tom Cruise's Fat-Suit Fracas," MSNBC.com, November 19, 2007.

285 Pamela McClintock, "Tropical Punch," *Variety*, August 18, 2008.

286 *Tropic Thunder* DVD

287 *Ibid.*

288 Cal Fussman, "Tom Cruise: The Fixer," *Esquire*, June 7, 2010.

289 Ray Greene, "Man with a Mission," *Boxoffice*, April 1996.

290 *Ibid.*

291 *Ibid.*

292 *Ibid.*

293 Geoff Boucher, "*Mission: Impossible*: Brad Bird Goes into Cruise Control," *Los Angeles Times*, November 2, 2011.

294 "Mogul on a Mission," *Variety*, May 7, 2008.

295 *Mission: Impossible— Ghost Protocol* press notes, 2011.

296 *Ibid.*

297 George Christy, "The Great Life," *Hollywood Reporter*, September 24, 1996.

298 Michael Fleming, "Tom Cruise," *Playboy*, June 2012.

299 *Ibid.*

300 Sean Smith, "Fear Factor," *Newsweek*, June 27, 2005.

301 "Spy," *Hello!* October 18, 2010

302 Michael Fleming, *op. cit.*

303 *Mission: Impossible— Ghost Protocol* press notes, *op. cit.*

304 Michael Fleming, *op. cit.*

305 Geoff Boucher, "Tom Cruise Has Fervent Fan in *Mission: Impossible* Director," *Los Angeles Times*, September 29, 2011.

306 Nick Pinkerton, "Man on a Mission," *Village Voice*, December 14, 2011.

307 Manohla Dargis, "Falling Off Skyscrapers Sometimes Hurts a Bit," *The New York Times*, December 15, 2011.

308 Michael Fleming, *op. cit.*

309 David Rensin, *op. cit.*

310 *Ibid.*

311 *Top Gun* press notes, 1986.

312 Lynn Hirschberg, "Conversation," *op. cit.*

313 Ray Greene, *op. cit.*

314 David Rensin, *op. cit.*

315 *Ibid.*

316 *Top Gun* press notes, 1986.

317 Lynn Hirschberg, "*Conversation,*" *op. cit.*

318 Ray Greene, *op. cit.*

Sidebars

a Rob Lowe, *op. cit.*

b "Morning Report," *Los Angeles Times*, December 9, 1987.

c H. G. Reza, "Tailhook Leaders Hope to Renew Ties with the Navy," *Los Angeles Times*, August 24, 1992.

d Jesse Kornbluth, "Cruise Control," *Vanity Fair*, January 1989.

e Michael Atkinson, "Icon See Clearly Now," *Village Voice*, December 11, 2001.

f Nancy Collins, "Lust & Trust," *Rolling Stone*, July 8, 1999.

g David Thomson, *Nicole Kidman, New York: Vintage*, 2008.

h Gary Susman, "War of the Words," *The Boston Phoenix*, July 1, 2005.

i "Tom Cruise Opens Up About His Beliefs in the Church of Scientology," *Der Spiegel*, April 27, 2005.

j Andrew Purvis, "Why Germany Hates Tom Cruise," *Time*, June 26, 2007.

k *Der Spiegel, op. cit.*

l David Thomson, "*Magnolia,*" *The Independent*, February 20, 2000.

m Anthony Lane, "Save Us," *The New Yorker*, May 15, 2006.

n Seven Mcdonald, "Tom Tom Club," *LA Weekly, May 12, 2006.*

o "A One Story Town," *Cougar Town*, March 13, 2012.

p Carla Hay, "Ben Stiller and *The Watch* Co-Stars Combat Aliens in This Sci-fi Comedy," *Examiner*, June 14, 2013.

Original title: *Tom Cruise*
© 2014 Cahiers du cinéma
SARL

Titre original:
Tom Cruise © 2014
Cahiers du cinéma SARL

This Edition published by
Phaidon Press Limited
under licence from Cahiers
du cinéma SARL,
18-20, rue Claude-Tillier,
75012 Paris, France © 2014
Cahiers du cinéma SARL.

Cette Édition est publiée
par Phaidon Press Limited
avec l'autorisation des
Cahiers du cinéma SARL,
18-20, rue Claude-Tillier,
75012 Paris, France © 2014
Cahiers du cinéma SARL.

Cahiers du cinéma
18-20, rue Claude-Tillier
75012 Paris

www.cahiersducinema.com

ISBN: 978 0 7148 6801 1

A CIP catalogue record of this
book is available from the
British Library.

Series concept designed
by Thomas Mayfried
Designed by Line Célo

Printed in China

Acknowledgments

This book would have been
impossible without the
Academy of Motion Picture
Arts and Sciences' Margaret
Herrick Library. My
gratitude to its archivists
and clerks, plus my favorite
security guard, Corliss Rauls.
Thanks to the friends
and colleagues who peppered
me with Tom Cruise
fun facts, especially those
I repurposed as unpaid
editors: Jen Yamato, Inkoo
Kang, Eva Anderson,
Christy Lemire, Josh Dickey,
Jack Giroux, Jeremy Smith,
and Scott Jordan Harris.
Above all, thank you
to my inspiration, Karina
Longworth; and a special
thank-you to my coach,
champion, and comrade,
Devin Faraci, who tracked
down a VHS tape of Tom
Cruise's forgotten directorial
debut and even convinced me
to write the *Eyes Wide Shut*
chapter at Kubrick's Stanley
Hotel.

Photographic credits

©AP Photo/Chris Pizzello/Sipa Press:
p. 144; © Photo by David Fisher/Rex
Features/Sipa Press: cover; Alfred A.
Knopf, 1976: p. 67; Archives du 7ᵉ Art/
DR/Photo12: p. 8, 32, 78; Archives
du 7ᵉ Art/Legend Production Company/
Photo12: p. 14 (t); Archives du 7ᵉ Art/
New Line Cinema/Photo12: p. 154 (t);
Archives du 7e Art/Paramount Pictures:
p. 41 (b); Archives du 7ᵉ Art/Paramount
Pictures/Photo12: p. 35, 122; Archives
du 7e Art/The Geffen Company/
Photo12: p. 20 (b), 22-23; Collection
Cahiers du cinéma: p. 108, 178 (tr), 182;
Collection Cahiers du cinéma/2008
United Artists Production Finance, LLC.
All rights reserved: p. 14 (b); Collection
CAT'S – Paramount Pictures: p. 150-
151; Collection Christophel: p. 178 (bl),
178 (br); Collection Christophel/
Paramount Pictures: p. 81; Collection
Christophel/Twentieth Century Fox:
p. 9; Columbia TriStar: p. 82, 85, 92;
Columbia TriStar/Collection Cahiers
du cinéma: p. 80; Columbia TriStar/tcd:
p. 90-91; Columbia TriStar/The Kobal
Collection/Andrew Cooper: p. 83;
Dreamworks Llc: p. 148, 149; Geffen
Pictures: p. 69; Geffen Pictures/
Collection Cahiers du cinéma: p. 64,
74 (t, b); Geffen Pictures/Collection
Christophel: p. 70-71, 72 73, 75, 77;
J.J. Guillèn/epa/Corbis: p. 130; Matt
Sayles/AP/Sipa Press: p. 154 (b); MTV
Movie Awards: p. 146; Neal Preston/
Corbis: p. 172-173; NBC/Getty Images
North America/Getty Images/AFP: p.
145; New Line: p. 115, 116, 117, 118,
120, 121, 122; New Line/Collection
Cahiers du cinéma: p. 112; Paramount
Pictures: p. 42, 47, 134, 136, 141, 153,
163, 169; Paramount Pictures/Collection
Cahiers du cinéma: p. 126, 156, 159,
160-161, 166-167, 174 (bl); Paramount
Pictures/Collection Christophel: p. 34,
36, 38-39, 44-45, 127, 128-129, 131,
132, 133 (t, b), 135, 138-139, 165,
168; Paramount Pictures/The Kobal
Collection: p. 41 (t), 43; Photo12/DR:
p. 30; Photo12.com – Collection
Cinéma/Warner Bros.: p. 107; Photo12/
TriStar Pictures: p. 86-87, 89; Prod.
DB © Touchstone Pictures/DR: p. 10-11;
The Kobal Collection/Dreamworks Llc:
p. 142; Tiberius/Tijuana/The Kobal
Collection: p. 18; Touchstone/Collection
Christophel: p. 174 (tr), 178 (tl); TriStar
Pictures/Collection; Christophel: p. 93;
Twentieth Century Fox/Photo12/DR:
p 13; Twentieth Century Fox/The Kobal
Collection: p. 12, 174 (tl); Universal:
p. 51; Universal/CAT'S: p. 60; Universal/
Collection Cahiers du cinéma: p. 48,
52-53, 58-59, 61, 62, 63; Universal/
Collection Christophel: p. 56, 174 (br);
Universal/Photo12: p. 55; Warner Bros.:
p. 24, 27, 101, 102, 106; Warner Bros./
Archives du 7e Art/DR/Photo12: p. 16;
Warner Bros./Collection Cahiers
du cinéma: p. 94, 97 (t), 98-99, 100,
104-105, 110, 111; Warner Bros./
Collection Christophel: p. 6, 20 (t), 31,
97 (b), 103; Warner Bros./The Kobal
Collection: p. 19, 28-29.

All reasonable efforts have been made
to trace the copyright holders of
the photographs used in this book.
We apologize to anyone that we were
unable to reach.

Cover illustration
Tom Cruise in 2012.